Trumpet Technique

TRUMPET TECHNIQUE

Frank Gabriel Campos

OXFORD
UNIVERSITY PRESS
2005

OXFORD
UNIVERSITY PRESS

Oxford New York

Auckland Bangkok Buenos Aires Cape Town Chennai
Dar es Salaam Delhi Hong Kong Istanbul Karachi Kolkata
Kuala Lumpur Madrid Melbourne Mexico City Mumbai
Nairobi São Paulo Shanghai Taipei Tokyo Toronto

Published by Oxford University Press, Inc.
198 Madison Avenue, New York, New York 10016

www.oup.com

Library of Congress Cataloging-in-Publication Data
Campos, Frank Gabriel.
Trumpet technique / Frank Gabriel Campos.
p. cm.
ISBN 0-19-516692-2; 0-19-516693-0 (pbk.)
1. Trumpet—Instruction and study. I. Title.
MT440 .C35 2004
788.9'2193—dc22 2004002576

1 3 5 7 9 8 6 4 2

Printed in the United States of America
on acid-free paper

For Sharon, Laura, and Leslie

ACKNOWLEDGMENTS

Portions of the text, including "A Letter to My Students," first appeared in the *International Trumpet Guild Journal*. My sincere thanks to current editor Gary Mortenson for permission to reproduce that material.

I am indebted to my good friend Ralph T. Dudgeon for his careful review of the manuscript and valuable suggestions, and to Arthur E. Ostrander and Ithaca College for the gift of two productive sabbaticals.

To my trumpet teachers John James Haynie, Leonard Candelaria, Don Jacoby, W. Ritchie Clendenin, James Stamp, Carole Klein, and my father, as well as many others who helped along the way, I owe a lifetime of thanks.

To my parents, Frank and Betty Campos, there are not thanks enough.

To Sharon, whose love is constant and true, and our beautiful daughters, Laura and Leslie, I dedicate this work.

CONTENTS

The moment one definitely commits oneself, then providence moves too. All sorts of things occur to help one that would never otherwise have occurred. A whole stream of events issues from the decision, raising in one's favor all manner of unforeseen incidents, meetings, and material assistance which no man could have dreamed would have come his way. Whatever you can do or dream you can, begin it. Boldness has genius, power, and magic in it. Begin it now.

—Johann Wolfgang von Goethe

If not now, when?

—Zen koan

Introduction

Technical skill determines our success in artistic performance to a larger degree than any single factor. Without it, the world's greatest artist would have nothing more to say than the average person in the street. Although making music can be a deeply satisfying thing to do, it can also be frustrating if you have difficulty expressing yourself because of such factors as an inadequate level of skill, poor technique, and fear.

Dedicated performers work their entire lives to develop their technique, not for its own sake, but to reach a higher level of expression. Correct technique usually manifests itself when we have a clear idea of the sound we want, but making improvements to technique is a normal part of a performer's life. In the pursuit of improved skill, success lies in the application of ideas that are based on natural laws and common sense. There are no hidden secrets, no cure-alls, and no shortcuts. A surprising number of trumpet players have difficulties that are caused by widespread misconceptions about the use of the body in performance.

The newer fields of sport science and sport psychology have yielded techniques that are directly applicable to the performing arts, and it was one of my primary goals to make them better known. Much of the material in this book applies to all brass and wind instrumentalists, and performing artists in other disciplines may find the chapters on skill acquisition, body use, and performance psychology useful.

Today, we gorge ourselves on huge amounts of information but rarely take the time to put a new idea into use. There is great potential for improvement within these pages, but to reap any benefit, you must act. Ideas about improving performance technique have no real value until they are applied in the practice room.

Is there a ceiling to your potential? Research tells us it is more likely that a decline in performance will occur with age or a change in motivation before you reach your limit. What really determines how well you perform is how much time you devote to it; regularly playing the instrument is the single most important factor in skill development. If you enjoy playing and always try to play beautifully and musically, you will grow by leaps and bounds. Remember that you can only move toward your goals and change your life in the present moment. What you choose now will determine who you will be in five, ten, or twenty years.

1

The Nature of Skill

The Dilettante and the Pedant

Skilled performance is the medium through which an artist communicates. The only purpose of skill is to convey a message, yet to a great extent, skill determines our success as performers.

The transformation of an immature student to a mature artist depends largely on the acquisition of skill. We can better understand the relationship of skill to artistic expression by examining performers from opposite ends of the spectrum: the dilettante and the pedant.

Perhaps lacking the discipline or interest to master the medium, the dilettante is a person with an interest in artistic performance who has, at best, mediocre skills. The dilettante might have something worthwhile to say, but without skill, s/he cannot communicate it to others.

The pedant, on the other hand, slavishly works to acquire technique for its own sake. The pedant may practice for hours on end to achieve perfection, but the result is without heart because s/he mistakes an empty display of skill for the elevated or sublime.

The dilettante and the pedant are unbalanced performers because of too little or, ironically, too much dependence on skill. In both cases, skill plays a dominant role in artistic communication. Most performing artists lie somewhere on the spectrum between the unskilled person with a message and the skilled person with no message. Those who lack both skill and message learn to find another line of work. The rare performer of great skill with something wonderful to say is the model that we should emulate.

A Definition of Skill

What exactly is skill? The dictionary describes it as "proficiency," "dexterity in the execution of learned tasks," or "the ability to use knowledge effectively in doing something." Researcher Harry Johnson defined skill as "the ability to execute a pattern of behavioral elements in proper relation to a certain environment" (Johnson 1961, 163). A skill is not a reflex action; it is a complex movement that requires practice. To fully understand skill in musical performance, we need a definition that is more specific.

Skill can refer to the general ability to do a thing, such as play the trumpet, or to an aspect of that skill, such as the ability to produce a beautiful tone. It could also refer to your level of proficiency, such as how well you perform. Skill is relative, meaning that you may be considered a highly skilled performer in your small town but not in a big city. In addition, a given task may rely more heavily on one type of skill than another, such as motor (muscle) skill or cognitive (mental) skill. For example, you may be able to multiple tongue rapidly but be a poor sight reader. Skills that we develop naturally through maturation, such as walking and talking, are called *phylogenetic* skills. Skills that we learn through practice and experience, such as reading, writing, or playing a musical instrument, are called *ontogenetic* skills. There are several other classifications of skill—far more than can be covered here—but one point is clear: it is difficult to arrive at an exact definition of skill.

The two very general areas of skill that we will be most concerned with in this chapter are motor skill and cognitive skill. Motor skill may be defined as the muscular activity directed toward a specific goal or objective, and cognitive skill is mental activity such as comprehending, organizing, analyzing, synthesizing, evaluating, and interpreting. Performing artists rely on both motor and cognitive skills in different degrees depending on the specific task. The cognitive and motor domains are inseparable when we play a musical instrument, so the terms *psychomotor, sensorimotor,* and *perceptualmotor* are generally used to refer to the role of the mind, nerves, and senses. (The affective domain, which refers to emotions, attitudes and values, will be covered in chapter 6.)

Three Models of Skill

What are the component parts of skilled performance? An examination of the similarities and differences between three very different models by Harry W. Johnson, Donald A. Norman, and John Sloboda will help us understand the possible variables and arrive at a model of skill for the performing artist.

Harry W. Johnson's Model of Skill

According to researcher Harry W. Johnson in the article "Skill = Speed x Accuracy x Form x Adaptability," skill is "the ability to execute a pattern of behavioral elements in proper relation to a certain environment" (1961, 163). To help the reader better understand the behavioral elements he refers to, Johnson recounts the "Woodchopper's Ball," a fabled contest of skill between a Swede and a Finn to determine who was the greatest lumberjack of all. The men were first judged for their speed in chopping a cord of wood; when they finished in a draw, the judges decided to test the accuracy of the contestants. After splitting matchsticks and straws with equal precision, the judges decided that the man with the best form, or the most efficient axe handler, would be declared the winner. They were challenged to see who could chop for the longest period, but after a few hours the men dropped to the ground in exhaustion at the same moment. Finally, a test of adaptability was proposed. In this contest, the men were asked to chop under varying conditions. After splitting many kinds of wood with different axes on chopping blocks of nonstandard height, the Swede was declared the winner, for "without his own ax and block, the Finlander was an ordinary man" (166).

According to Johnson, then, skill can be judged by observing speed, accuracy, form, and adaptability. Before we comment on whether this is a good model to use in the evaluation of artistic skill, let us look at some other theories.

Donald A. Norman's Model of Skill

According to psychologist Donald A. Norman in *Learning and Memory* (1982), five variables separate the performance of a skilled performer from a performer of lesser skill. Those variables are:

1. *Smoothness*, or the ability to perform a task with ease, grace, and efficiency. A skilled performer uses less effort

to perform and, compared to the amateur, makes it look easy.

2. *Automaticity,* or the ability to perform a task without knowing what one is doing. While playing an instrument, for example, the skilled performer is not consciously aware of what his/her fingers are doing while making music. The physical motions have been practiced until they are automatic.
3. A skilled performer has the ability to perform a task with *little or no mental effort.* S/he has no need to mentally monitor each action, and that reduces the mental workload. "As skill increases, mental effort decreases" (Norman, 72).
4. The ability to perform a task with *no significant deterioration of skill due to stress* is a characteristic of highly skilled performers. This is probably due to the fact that the behavior is automated and requires little mental effort. "The responses to a stressful situation may already have been learned, practiced, and perhaps even made automatic" (Norman, 73).
5. *Point of view* is the ability to attend to a variety of tasks while focusing on a single goal or objective. As a performer gains skill, his/her point of view moves from attending to many individual tasks to simply making music. The instrument becomes an extension of the body, and the performer focuses on the product s/he desires.

The theoretical models of skill as proposed by Johnson and Norman overlap to some degree, yet each has distinct elements. Let's look at yet another model.

John A. Sloboda's Model of Skill

In a chapter titled "What Is Skill?" (Gellatly 1986), John A. Sloboda proposes that the characteristics of skilled performance include fluency, rapidity, automaticity, simultaneity, and knowledge.

Fluency refers to the way individual components work together in a smooth, integrated sequence. According to Sloboda, when we are moving fluently, we blend a sequence of movements so that they overlap in time. In other words, the movements in preparation for a second motion happen while the first motion is still occurring. In addition, fluent performers can "chunk" many actions into a set that can be used as a single motion. Sloboda believes that fluency is the last aspect of skilled behavior to be acquired.

A skilled performer is able to make the appropriate responses with *rapidity*. This is because a skilled performer's knowledge and experience allows him/her to detect patterns that a less skilled performer cannot perceive. "It is the ability to make the right response almost immediately that is so characteristic of all skill" (Sloboda, 19).

Automaticity, or automatic behavior, is the same characteristic that Norman refers to, but Sloboda's description makes reference to the idea of "lack of mental effort," as well as the concept of efficiency in his definition. Sloboda also states that automatic behavior is generally "mandatory," meaning that it must follow the path that is learned.

Simultaneity is similar to Norman's *point of view:* a skilled performer is able to accomplish several tasks at once without conscious attention. (He also mentions *automaticity* and the ability to function without mental monitoring.) Sloboda notes that psychologists are not sure whether our attention is capable of being divided or whether we simply move it rapidly between tasks, but research shows that the brain cannot think more than one thought at a time. When attending to two or more tasks, our attention moves rapidly from thought to thought, giving the impression of having more than one thought at once. This is a moot point with automatic behavior since it requires little or no mental monitoring, but the ability to switch one's attention rapidly between tasks is a characteristic of an elite performer. (See "Attention and Concentration" in chapter 6.)

Knowledge seems a logical component of skilled performance, but Sloboda makes the point that knowledge is of no use if it is not available when it is needed. A skilled musician, for instance, will not be able to demonstrate anything without his/her instrument in hand or if s/he is not in the context in which the knowledge needs to be applied. Knowledge is usually associated with situations through training and experience. Most performing artists receive extensive schooling in institutions or with master performers and teachers, but the knowledge gained through experience has the most value to the mature performer.

The apparent lack of agreement between researchers on a working definition of the characteristics of skilled performance is due in large part to the wide diversity of behavior we call skilled. Some scientists have been criticized for attempting to apply the results of laboratory research that studied very simple skills with no resemblance to the complexities of artistic performance.

The Six Characteristics of Skill

We have seen that skill is composed of many characteristics woven together in a tapestry, with each element dependent upon the others. What are the elements of skill in the performing arts? With the understanding that naming them individually is an illusion of separation, I would submit that they are these six: efficiency, automaticity, timing, knowledge, adaptability, and capacity.

Efficiency is the ability to perform with economy and an apparent lack of physical effort. In this definition, we include Norman's *smoothness* and Sloboda's *rapidity* since efficient performance implies the ability to perform a task quickly with fluency, smoothness, and grace. Since the most efficient form is the best possible form, we also include Johnson's *form*. It is impossible to say whether one aspect of skilled performance is more important than the others, but efficiency is the bed in which most of them lie. Without efficiency, we are not using the best form and technique for the job, and that will significantly alter the message we wish to convey.

Automaticity is the ability to perform without conscious awareness, mental effort, or monitoring. This definition encompasses Sloboda's *simultaneity* and Norman's *point of view*. It is without a doubt one of the most important components of skill, for without automatic behavior we would be required to constantly monitor actions we take for granted. To know how it feels to have to consciously monitor many tasks at once, recall your first attempts to ride a bike.

Timing is the ability to do something at the proper moment and in the proper sequence. Like efficiency, this component of skill implies *smoothness*, grace, fluidity, and *rapidity*, but the ability to do a thing precisely when it is required is not inherent in any of these characteristics. Timing is the part of musical skill that allows us to coordinate our actions within the matrix of time. Without it, we would not be able to play together with other musicians. Timing allows a batter to swing and hit the ball at precisely the right moment and a musician to play a rhythm at the proper tempo.

Knowledge is required to understand music and the musical world, and to make music with other musicians. It is also needed to achieve and maintain a high degree of personal skill, such as knowing what and how to practice. Remember that much of the knowledge used in high-level skill must be associated to very specific situations to be demonstrated and may be of no particular use in another context. For example, a highly skilled classical musician might be unable to demonstrate his/her skill in a jazz setting. Knowledge may take the form of experience, such as knowing the different styles and protocols for a given musical genre, or as learned cognitive skills, such as the ability to transpose, sight-read, or improvise over chord changes. It also includes knowing how to survive as a professional musician in a competitive environment.

Adaptability is the ability to perform under diverse (and especially adverse) circumstances. If an artist is unable to cope with the performing environment, then high-level performance is not possible. This could be considered an aspect of automaticity, but automatic behavior can break down in certain circumstances. Stress, sleep deprivation, fatigue, fear, over- or underarousal, and other factors play a big part in how one is able to perform. Remember that Johnson's Finn, whose skill was a match for the Swede in every way, lost the contest because he could not adapt to new equipment. In *The Art of Brass Playing* (1962), Phillip Farkas makes reference to "warm-up artists" who are able to play with incredible ability in the practice room but cannot function in a performance environment where stresses are very high. Ideally, we want automatic behaviors to be so strong that they override stressors.

Capacity refers to the mental, physical, emotional and artistic requirements necessary to perform with great skill as well as to one's aptitude for a particular task. Performers whose physical or mental capabilities prevent them from fully expressing themselves are too common: a pianist with small hands, an oboist with asthma, or a singer with severe performance anxiety. Sometimes these deficiencies can be overcome with determination and hard work, but not always. Whether one is predisposed to play a given instrument is a question that is usually determined on an individual basis. There are factors which play a dominant role in the success of those who might not ordinarily "fit the profile," including determination and desire, but there is no denying that not everyone is destined to play first chair.

The Question of Talent

An individual's artistic capacity, or talent, is of supreme importance in the arts. I originally considered *artistry* as a seventh area of skill but determined that it fits within the domain of *capacity*. Some individuals seem to have a greater capacity to express themselves artistically than others, but researchers still question whether there exists a genetic predisposition for a certain activity, or whether factors like practice and desire play the largest role. Do we have to be born with the ability to be an artist or can it be taught? Anders Ericsson (1993) and his colleagues have put forth the theory that ten years of optimal deliberate practice will produce expertise in most fields (including music) and that environmental factors, not inherited traits or talent, are the primary predictors of success. These environmental factors include the proper learning resources, strong motivation, and effort.

Ericsson's Deliberate Practice Theory is a highly controversial point of view, but there is little evidence to disqualify it and much to support it. Consider the following, taken from Kirschenbaum (1997): most prodigies do not become exceptional adult performers; chess grand masters have an average IQ equal to the average college student; the reaction and hand speed of expert and nonexpert pianists of similar age in one study were measured to be the same; in a similar study, experts in tennis, chess, typing, and other fields showed superior cognitive or memory skill only in their field of expertise. The only area where expert performers consistently and significantly differ from nonexpert performers is in the intensity and amount of their practice.

Is artistry a matter of talent and giftedness, or can it be learned? James Thurmond's excellent *Note Grouping* (1982) has shown that it is possible to teach a student to perform with expression, style, and musicianship by studying and imitating the interpretive choices of the greatest artists. A student who is fundamentally unable to play with steady time or accurate pitch may lack the capacity to be successful at the highest levels, but given the inspiring stories of individuals who have overcome tremendous adversity to succeed, I would not rule anyone out. A dedicated teacher will usually do all in his/her power to help a sincere student, but the responsibility for success lies primarily in the student's hands. A teacher should not make the mistake of calling a duck a swan by exaggerating a student's ability, nor destroy a student's dreams by imposing limited expectations. This is often a difficult line to walk.

A full discussion of the question of environment versus heredity is beyond the scope of this book, as is the question of what makes an artist. For the interested reader who may wish to pursue this topic further, Howard Gardner's *Theory of Multiple Intelligences* (1983) and the writing of Françoys Gagné on talent are a good starting point.

Efficiency: The Primary Goal

If there is a single quality of physical skill that ranks in importance above all others, it is efficiency. It is the very heart of high-level motor skill. Accomplished performers spend most of their practice time refining their skill in order to perform more efficiently. To refine means to separate what is undesired from what is desired, producing a product that is pure and unadulterated. In physical performance skill, we seek to eliminate excessive tension, for the presence of excess tension separates the amateur from the expert. It is not an easy or quick process, but it is the only path to mastery.

Efficiency is intertwined with other qualities. The efficient performer's movements are fluent, with each individual movement blended into a whole. As we learn to do a task more efficiently, we are able to do it more rapidly. (Observe a beginner trying to perform a passage that calls for speed and you'll see why this is a characteristic of the expert.) Speed is a subset of timing, or the ability to do the right thing at the right moment in the right sequence. Efficient movements are almost always automatic, but this does not mean that automatic behavior is always efficient; it is just as easy to learn to do something the wrong way as it is to do it correctly.

Efficiency is absolutely dependent on one's physical capacity. We cannot perform at the highest level when sick, injured, or out of shape. Similarly, when we become fatigued we tend to make more errors, just as when we are pressed to do a task faster than we are able. An efficient performer can perform a task with more speed and accuracy than a less efficient performer, but in trying to save energy by going very slowly, it is possible to use too little effort to meet the task, and ironically this is also inefficient.

According to Laban and Lawrence in their book *Effort* (1947), individuals who have a natural capacity for efficiency within a particular domain, or who have acquired a high degree of efficiency through experience in that field, may be just as awkward as any unskilled person when approaching tasks outside their arena of ability. An athlete who is predisposed to basketball, for example, may not be a particularly distinguished baseball player.

Efficiency is important because our lives are defined by time and energy. The performer who is most in control of these two elements will probably be the most successful. Of two musicians of equal physical strength—one who is an efficient performer and one who is not—the inefficient player will work much harder to perform a given piece and will become fatigued sooner. If the piece is long enough, s/he might even lack the energy to finish. The efficient performer has more available energy to accomplish the task and will more likely perform with greater accuracy and ease of expression.

Refining Skill

We waste effort through inappropriate movement during the execution of a given task, but how do we know what is appropriate movement? The true value of practice is that it allows us to eliminate movements that are a waste of energy. Our practice must be directed toward refining a task to its essence, but great amounts of practice may not necessarily contribute to that goal: even the most earnest and sincere efforts are of little value if they are not done with the specific goal of refinement.

When a new skill is learned, the initial attempts are usually very inefficient because the body is using more muscles than are needed. In fact, a beginner's muscles work in opposition to one another in a haphazard fashion. As we practice over time, we begin to refine muscle use by isolating and reinforcing the necessary ones and eliminating the unnecessary ones. As our form improves, we may even discover more effective muscles to do the job.

Learning to become more efficient is a constantly evolving process during which we actively try things based upon what we believe to be right. Using the results as our guide, we then reinforce what works and discard what does not. As John Holt said, "We learn to do something by doing it. There is no other way."

The Psychology of Learning

Psychomotor skill learning has been defined as a relatively permanent change in behavior that occurs due to practice or experience. Note that learning itself cannot be observed, but only inferred by the difference in the learner's behavior prior to and after training. Although research on skill acquisition dates from the late 1800s, there is still no single theory that explains how human beings acquire knowledge and skill. This is due in part to the dozens of variables that must be considered when we try to understand what happens in a particular learning situation, and every situation is different. (For more on skill acquisition and motor skill learning, see Singer et al., 2001.)

Traditional learning models such as operant conditioning and classical conditioning play an important part in the development of psychomotor skill, but it is *observational learning*, or the study of how we learn through observation and modeling, that most closely explains how performing artists acquire skill.

Observational Learning

According to Albert Bandura (1969), the four stages of observational learning are *attention*, *memory*, *reproduction*, and *motivation*. For example, attention refers to the keen interest a student takes in the skill of a master artist. The student uses memory to retain aspects of the artist's performance for the purpose of attempting to reproduce them during practice, and motivation keeps the student working until the goal of imitating the artist has been met.

Bandura's theories have been concerned with the acquisition of athletic skill through visual means, but musicians primarily use the aural sense to learn musical skill. Substituting the auditory rather than visual sense as the primary learning mode in observational learning does not change or invalidate Bandura's theory. In fact, his theory as applied to the acquisition of musical skill through auditory observation may even be a stronger model than that of visual observation of athletic skill.

The acquisition of artistic skill through observational learning requires a model, the motivation to be like the model, and the use of imitation and trial-and-error learning techniques. Although they are simple enough that a newborn uses them, these principles govern the learning of the most complex skills. In addition, we must add practice, which is the structured process of reinforcing new behaviors; goals, which are the direction and endpoints we establish; and feedback, which tells us whether we are moving toward our goals.

Imitation of the Model

Imitation is the most natural way to learn. From birth, we imitate what we see and hear around us. This process of imitative learning requires a learner and a model. The model is the example, the end result, the process in action, and the embodiment of the learner's goals, whether the goals are conscious or unconscious.

Who have been your models? They are most often individuals who have been close to you, such as parents and teachers, and sometimes they are world-class artists whose performances are only accessible through recordings. We have all heard stories about individuals whose lives have been changed by a single person. Miles Davis, who had one of the most unique and recognizable sounds in recorded history, has said he tried his entire life to emulate the sound of Freddie Webster, a relatively unknown trumpet player that the young Miles admired. In my life, the memories of the beautiful sound and expression of my undergraduate trumpet teacher, W. Ritchie Clendenin, influence my playing to this day. In addition, I might not have chosen the trumpet at all if my father had not played it.

Young children have little say in their choice of models, but when we mature we consciously choose them. For an aspiring artist, the most logical choice is someone who is very proficient at the task s/he desires to learn. Compared to virtually any other system or philosophy of education, imitation of a good model is the most effective way to learn and refine psychomotor skill.

According to Bandura, anything that can be learned from direct experience can be learned from observation. When we are exposed to behaviors we wish to acquire, we create and store images in the mind. Mental imaging is a natural function that human beings use constantly. These images are used as a pattern for the things we wish to learn. Studies have shown that by creating images in our imagination using more than one sense, such as visual, aural, and kinesthetic, we can more quickly produce the desired result. (See "Visualization" in chapter 6.)

Musical Interpretation and Concept of Sound

Imitating fine performers is one of the most important tasks in our musical development. Without a clear conception of sound and musical interpretation, beautiful playing is not possible. Often a student is able to sing musically with the voice, but on the trumpet, the interpretation is mechanical or unpleasant, as if the instrument presents a barrier to expression. When this occurs, ask the student to sing the phrase vocally and then play it on the instrument, observing the ways these two interpretations are different. The finest performers have their sound and expression clearly conceived. The correct playing technique will usually manifest itself when you have the desired sound clearly in your mind and insist on it every time you play.

When taking a lesson from a fine player, really listen closely to his/her sound and then try to play the same passage or note. Is your sound exactly the same? Become intensely aware of your sound and without trying to do anything specific, make it more like your teacher's. Keep listening and imitating using the trial-and-error process. Don't be frustrated or impatient, don't judge or analyze; just keep your attention on the sound. Your teacher may direct your attention to aspects or qualities of your sound or his/her sound that you may not have noticed. Your sound will soon undergo a change as you do this exercise, but you will probably not know exactly what made your sound change. When the physical processes are at the service of the imagination, miraculous things happen.

Always use the sound as your primary guide when experimenting with physical improvements to technique. A faulty conception of sound, however, will lead a student away from the most efficient way to play.

Trial and Error

Trial and error means to attempt and fail. It is an axiom of life that learning requires failure, but we often forget this. Each time we try and fail, we learn something that moves us closer to our goal. According to psychologist Edward L. Thorndike, trial and error is the most basic form of learning. It is the way we learn to walk, talk, sing, dance, or play an instrument.

Learning is as much a matter of eliminating what is not correct as strengthening what is correct. Through the results of our trials, we can begin to distinguish the elements of good form. Trial-and-error practice has three parts: we must repeat the behavior that we wish to acquire, constantly compare our results to the model or mental image, and correct any errors as they are detected.

When we learn by trial and error without adequate feedback about our progress from a teacher or observer, we run the risk of learning incorrect technique. Errors must be eliminated at the earliest possible stage in order to avoid reinforcing them. If we have a well-formed concept of our goals provided by an appropriate model, however, we can usually stay on course. (See "Feedback and Expectation" in this chapter.)

Product, Not Process

The skills that a performing artist must acquire are more easily and completely learned when we keep our attention on what we want rather than how we will do it, or as Arnold Jacobs put it, on "the product, not the process" (1987). (Timothy Gallwey addressed this point extensively in his *Inner Game of Tennis* [1974].) Turning a simple urge into action does not require an understanding of the means to accomplish the action. For example, to pick up your instrument, you do not need to know the names of the muscles, nor do you have to think about what your arm and hand must do in order reach and grasp—you just pick it up. Understanding the mechanisms necessary for the expression of purpose are of no more importance than needing to know exactly how the brain functions in order to think. When we want to sound like a particular artist, we need to imagine that person's sound, and without any specific direction to the body, perform trial after trial using the sound in our imagination as the guide. Soon our trials will begin to match the images we have focused our attention upon. It is truly remarkable that without any conscious effort, control, or oversight, the body will gradually make the changes necessary to move in the direction of the outcome we visualize. There are exceptions to this approach. (See "Remedial Work" in this chapter.)

Practice

Researchers generally agree that the single most important factor in skill acquisition is practice. Practice is structured repetition that results in learning. It is the way we learn any skill, simple or complex, and those who have achieved a significant level of accomplishment in any field know that there are no shortcuts. Some researchers believe that it takes about 1 million repetitions to attain skill mastery and a minimum of ten years of deliberate and optimal practice to reach the expert level in any given field of endeavor (Ericsson et al. 1993).

Although the point may seem self-evident to any experienced performer, research has shown a linear relationship between practice and expert performance, generally proving that the more one practices, the more skilled one becomes. Practice that is not goal directed and lacks feedback, however, has been shown to be worthless. Ashy and Landon (1988) studied the practice techniques of a group of fourth-grade soccer players. They found that the total amount of practice was not related to success unless correct technique was emphasized. The reinforcement of correct soccer technique contributed to success in performance ability, but the reinforcement of incorrect trials was regarded as a waste of time. It is clear that optimum practice involves minimizing incorrect trials and maximizing correct trials.

There has been a great deal of research by sports scientists in the area of practice, particularly in the investigation of the effectiveness of the particular ways we use practice time. Following are some areas that have received attention from researchers regarding how practice is structured.

Whole versus Part Practice

Observational learning theorists believe that we can learn a physical task just by observing and imitating the whole all at once, especially highly integrated tasks that are difficult to break into parts, but others believe that complex tasks should be learned in smaller units that are practiced separately and then integrated into the whole. The truth is that both of these ideas have value, and both have advantages and disadvantages depending on the learner and the task in question.

Whole learning promotes the smooth flow and critical timing that is the nature of high-level motor skill, but beginning learners may have great difficulty grasping all of the elements of a very complex task. A young pianist, for example, may need to spend time practicing each hand separately before putting them together. Part practice may help a beginner to master the elements of a complex task, but too much time spent reinforcing the individual parts may disconnect them from the flow of the whole and result in a product that is awkward or disjointed. In addition, when individual parts are practiced separately, they may be inadvertently executed differently from the way they should be executed as a part of the whole.

There is a compromise of the whole versus part that combines aspects of both, called the progressive-part approach. In this model, after one part of a task is learned, the second part is practiced along with the first, and then a third element is added. The process continues until the task is learned completely. This learning strategy allows the proper reinforcement of the parts but keeps the primary focus on the integration of the parts as a whole.

Some researchers believe that whole learning does not allow for the refinement necessary to reach the expert level and is therefore most effective for simpler skills. This may be true for visual imitation, but it is not true for aural imitation. Listening and imitating is the way that musicians acquire such subtle skills as conception of tone and musical interpretation. The observation and imitation of a master through aural means is the musician's primary learning mechanism.

Blocked versus Random Practice

Is it better to focus on one task for an entire practice session, such as scales, or to mix many tasks, such as scales, a sonata, and an etude? There is evidence that focusing on one task per session (blocked practice) produces poorer long-term learning retention than addressing many tasks in a session (random practice). There are two possible reasons. First, when a player is involved with several different tasks in one session, the memory must work harder to keep each task distinct and separate, which promotes better retention. Second, when a learner returns to a particular task after practicing others in a single session, s/he may have forgotten some of what was learned in earlier trials and must work harder to recall it, which leads to better memory retrieval. (Recent research, however, indicates that practicing a second new motor skill soon after learning the first can impede the retention of the first skill. See "Learning Breaks" in this chapter.)

While random practice appears to be a better practice strategy overall, there are many circumstances when the reinforcement of a single skill or task for a long period is the best choice. This kind of practice should not be ruled out, but rather used when the player feels it is necessary.

Constant versus Variable Practice

Is it better to practice a single skill or task under constant conditions or to make the practice conditions variable? For example, if a player is practicing scales, would it be better to practice them at the same dynamic level and with a single style of articulation, or should s/he practice various dynamics and articulations? If the idea of practice is to prepare for performance, then those conditions that most closely mimic real performance will be preferable. (See "Transfer of Learning" in this chapter.) Variable practice more easily transfers to real performance, whereas constant conditions may limit the variety of possible responses. Through variable practice, the learner develops flexible behavior patterns that allow quicker responses to the needs of the moment. The exception to this preference for variable practice is the beginning learner, who will benefit from a constant version of a skill or task until it has been learned. In this case, variable practice may be introduced after the basic skill has been mastered.

Distributed versus Massed Practice

One of the questions in psychological research that has received a great deal of attention in recent years is whether skills are best learned in a single, long practice session or in several shorter sessions. In other words, is it more effective to practice for three hours uninterrupted or to distribute that practice into three hour-long sessions? Although the issue is heavily debated with no firm answers, researchers agree that there is a difference in the resulting product and that each method is appropriate for certain kinds of tasks. A more definite answer is that massed practice is good for certain types of tasks, but for most situations distributed practice is preferred. Massed practice produces quicker results, but they are not retained as long as the results of distributed practice, which is slower but more durable. Distributed practice appears to be especially well suited to motor skill learning for several reasons. First, practicing for shorter periods will produce a greater number of repetitions that are close to perfect because they are not degraded by fatigue or boredom. Second, it is possible to maintain energy and intensity at a high level for shorter periods, which is especially important when practicing tasks that are labor-intensive. Third, motivation and attention are easier to maintain at a high level during short practice sessions.

Forward and Backward Chaining

Another area of skill acquisition that has received attention from researchers is the order in which the elements of a skill are taught. Teaching that progresses from the beginning of a skill movement sequence to its end point, as is the way it is most frequently done, is known as forward chaining. Certain skills, however, may be more effectively taught in reverse order, progressing from the end point to the beginning, a process called backward chaining.

When teaching a golf swing using the forward chaining technique, for example, instruction begins from the beginning of the stroke and proceeds forward step by step to the end, so that the learner is always progressing from the known, or that which has just been taught, to the unknown, or that which hasn't been taught yet. In backward chaining, instruction begins at the end point, or at the end of the stroke, and goes backward incrementally. In other words, the learner is instructed that the end or terminal position of the stroke will be attained every time the sequence is practiced. Each step of the sequence starts with the new element followed by the remainder of the skill which has already been successfully performed on previous trials, so that the skill is learned by teaching the last element of the skill first, then the last two, then the last three, and so on.

Backward chaining (BC) appears to have several definite advantages over forward chaining (FC). In BC, the learner always follows a newly learned element of the skill sequence with material that has already been performed successfully, but in FC the learner is always moving into unknown territory. As a result, FC tends to produce more errors than BC. BC tends to produce less tension and anxiety because of the greater probability of a high success rate in the learning and because it is simpler and easier for the student to grasp.

Although FC appears to have definite weaknesses compared to BC, its use as the predominant way we teach is not questioned. In examining other research, however, FC still has advantages under certain conditions. In a study by Ash and Holding (1990), participants who were asked to learn a piano piece using both BC and FC learned the piece better and more thoroughly using FC. Researchers believe that the nature of a given task is what makes one learning progression better than the other. In tasks that need a high degree of end-point accuracy, such as a tennis stroke or basketball layup, BC is superior. In tasks where all parts are equally critical to the success of the performance, such as a piece of music, FC is a more effective learning process. Certain aspects of artistic skill, however, may be unsuitable to either approach, such as when learning concept of sound and musical style.

I have found BC to be very helpful in learning complex note sequences. The technique consists of playing the last note, then the last two notes, and then the last three notes, slowly working backward step by step. This is a very effective technique for difficult passages since they fit to some degree the definition of the type of task that would be best learned through BC. Despite the findings of the study by Ash and Holding, BC is worth investigating as a teaching technique, particularly for single-note instruments like the trumpet. A student learning a piece this way could practice the last bar(s), then the next-to-last one(s), and so on. Younger players in particular may find this approach easier and perhaps more fun than FC.

Practice with Beans

Each year I give my new students a small plastic bag containing several dried beans and describe how Wolfgang Amadeus Mozart's father, Leopold, placed ten dried beans in his son's left coat pocket during young Mozart's practice. For every successful attempt of a difficult passage, Mozart would move a single bean to his right pocket. If he failed, even on the tenth trial, all of the beans would be placed back in the left pocket and he would have to begin again. Students who use this practice technique find that the only way to play ten correct trials in a row is to play very slowly, and that is what makes it invaluable.

The scientific principles behind this technique are described in "Mind, Muscle and Music" by Frank R. Wilson (1981). Wilson explains that the cerebellum regulates the timing and smoothness of muscular contractions, including learned sequences of precise and controlled movements such as those used in performance. These types of movements must first be learned slowly, ahead of time. According to Wilson, "[We work] out the details, step by step, making corrections when we observe our own mistakes . . . consciously and deliberately establishing patterns of movements . . . which eventually become less tentative, and finally become smooth and sure" (10). Wilson is describing the process of correct practice.

When a skill finally becomes automatic, it moves from the conscious part of the brain to the cerebellum, which functions like an automatic pilot. We are then free to put our attention on musical rather than physical concerns since the body is "programmed" to go through the patterns we have taught it. The cerebellum records the motor patterns that we repeat over and over in our practice, but it cannot make any distinction between right and wrong movements. If we carelessly rush through our practice without concern for accuracy, sound, time, or any of the other critical parameters of music, then these faults will be reflected in our performance. Therefore, if we want to learn a skill correctly, we must repeat it correctly, and that usually means practicing slowly, at least initially. Using beans is an excellent way to ensure that we are getting as much as possible out of our practice time.

Feedback and Expectations

The two most important factors in the development of high-level skill, in addition to practice, are feedback and motivation. (Motivation will be discussed in chapter 6.)

Research in the area of practice has conclusively established that a learner's skill acquisition is greatly facilitated by feedback about his/her progress. In general, the more specific and accurate the feedback, the faster the skill is learned. Feedback provides information about the success or failure of the learner's behavior, as well as information about the things that must be changed in order to move toward the goal of improved performance. The teacher must ensure that the learner has no questions about the work that needs to be done, what is expected, or how to do the work. The phrase that sums up this principle is "make your expectations clear."

Feedback should tell the learner about his/her success relative to the goal of a task (*knowledge of results*) and illuminate the success of a particular movement or technique (*knowledge of performance*). Studies have shown that when feedback indicates that the learner is significantly off target relative to the goal, the student's response may differ depending upon his/her level of self-confidence and motivation. A less motivated individual may reduce effort and persistence or even give up, but a highly motivated individual may increase effort and set new strategies or goals.

The accuracy, frequency, and timeliness of feedback affect its usefulness. In the early stages of skill learning, feedback should be provided frequently, but research shows that skill retention and transfer of learning are better when the frequency of feedback is lessened once an adequate level of ability has been achieved. Learners should not be allowed to become overly reliant on feedback.

Feedback is an essential part of the process of setting goals; goals and feedback are far more effective together than alone. (See "Goal Setting" in chapter 6.)

Transfer of Learning

In order for practice to have value, it must provide reinforcement of the skills needed in real performance. There must be a transfer of the learned material from practice to performance, and the greater the transfer, the quicker and more complete the acquisition of skill. The most important element affecting the positive transfer of learning is the similarity of the practice to performance. Researchers found that when practice and performance tasks are similar in structure, positive transfer occurs, but when they are dissimilar, the difference interferes with performance skill. In fact, practice that employs a large number of drills or exercises containing skill elements irrelevant to performance will lead to poor or incorrect skill execution. The greater the similarity of the drills and exercises to real performance, the more value practice will have in improving performance skill.

Making a learner very aware of the most important aspects of practice, as well as how and why things must be done to improve performance skill, will facilitate positive transfer. For example, telling a student that practicing scales is important is not enough; it would be better to emphasize the importance of the accuracy of attack, steady tempo, and beauty of sound. In addition, it is best to have the student focus on smaller and more manageable short-term goals that lead to long-term goals rather than always emphasizing the long-term objective.

Effective transfer from practice to performance requires an understanding and rehearsal of the cognitive (mental) aspects of performance. It is not sufficient to practice only the physical aspects of a skill; we must also reproduce the mental activity. Duplicating the conditions under which a learner will have to perform can help him/her overcome anxiety and provide an awareness of the need to improve mental discipline and focus. (See chapter 6.) Therefore, transfer of skill is most positively facilitated when practice is contextually, physically, and cognitively the same as performance; the value of practice decreases the more we depart from this principle.

Learning Breaks

Researchers at Johns Hopkins University found that learning a second motor skill too soon after learning the first impairs retention or even wipes out the first skill (Simon 1997). The results of this study conclusively showed that a delay of five to six hours is necessary between the learning of new motor skills to ensure complete retention. When a second skill was learned after a one-hour break, the subjects retained only a portion of the first skill. After five to six hours, however, the skill appeared to be completely imprinted in the brain. Although it may be inconvenient to implement this principle in the normal teaching environment, it is clear that for motor skill learning to be most effective, new skills must be given time to imprint.

Remedial Work

Inexperienced teachers typically spend too much time telling their students how to play, instead of showing them. Arnold Jacobs's phrase "product not process" refers to the importance of relying on musical images to guide our musical growth. When our attention is focused on the sounds we want, the body makes changes to the way we play in order to produce the results we imagine. We must let the body naturally figure out the necessary changes, not try to guide the process consciously. Focusing on the product rather than the process is the most efficient way to learn artistic skill, but there are some exceptions to this approach.

A student with a dysfunctional embouchure can spend years listening to and trying to sound like his/her teacher, but until s/he takes conscious steps to physically correct the embouchure, the problem will not be resolved. There is a time and place for specific instruction about physical performance; even Jacobs gave very explicit directions about bodily processes when it was appropriate to do so. It is not wrong to know a great deal about how the body works in skilled performance as long as that knowledge is used to diagnose and correct dysfunctional form. That is its only useful purpose.

Remedial teaching is the name for the process of correcting poor performance habits and retraining the learner with correct habits. The difficulty of remedial teaching is that the student already has well-established skills that will resist all attempts at eradication or change. Developmental teaching, or the teaching of new skills, suggests that the student is a blank slate upon which new skills are imprinted with no interference. Even with beginners, however, this is rarely the case because poor performance habits can quickly become established before the teacher is aware of them. The reality is that virtually all students require some type of remedial work, so every teacher needs to understand the process whereby we "unlearn" habits.

Replacing Bad Habits

The technical skill of the most accomplished performers in any field is fluid and free of the appearance of effort, but our first efforts to imitate them are usually labored and inefficient. Our form improves over time, but the goal of efficient performance is a life-long process. Even the finest performers have a few habitual movements, behaviors, or ways of thinking that could be improved. The process of replacing poor habits is an elemental task that every performer must learn, but there is confusion about the best way to go about it.

A habit, whether good or bad, is a conditioned response that has been established through reinforcement over a long period of time. We cannot change or unlearn habits; we must replace them with new ones. Once a habit is acquired, it is with us forever. Even when a bad habit fades through lack of use, it can return quickly when a player inadvertently reinforces it, even after many years.

When a habit has been identified as counterproductive to good performance, the average student usually begins trying to change it by sheer force of will. For example, if the student is in the habit of placing the mouthpiece too low on the embouchure, s/he will attempt to place it higher each time s/he plays. However, it is extremely difficult to replace a habit in this fashion. Established behaviors, whether good or bad, are automatic and their path is predetermined; they do not rely on conscious thought or will to initiate action. When the instrument is raised to the lips, the automatic behavior asserts itself, and a mighty struggle begins between the habit and the player's will to change the habit. This is not the best way to replace behavior. As Mark Twain said, "Habit is habit and not to be flung out of the window by any man, but coaxed downstairs a step at a time."

Introducing Strangeness

In psychological terms, the instrument is a *hot cue*: it strongly stimulates our preconditioned responses (established habits), so while the instrument is in our hands, it is extremely difficult to change the way we do things. In order to establish new habits, we first have to find a way to practice the new, desired behavior. It is best to do that away from the instrument where there are no habitual forces compelling established behavior. Arnold Jacobs said he short-circuited such conditioned responses by introducing *strangeness*. Strangeness is simply doing something familiar in a completely different or strange way. For example, a student who wants to place the mouthpiece higher on the embouchure is struggling because of the body's strong conditioned response to place it low. But by working with the mouthpiece alone rather than the whole instrument, the player may more easily put the mouthpiece in the correct position. S/he could start by holding it in the new position and buzzing simple tones. After many days of practicing the mouthpiece alone, the player will find that a new conditioned response is taking root. The new way of placing the mouthpiece on the embouchure will gain in strength, eventually becoming automatic, and the old behavior will begin to extinguish through lack of reinforcement. Even though the old habit is no longer a part of the player's technique, however, it is not completely gone: it could easily return if the player inadvertently began playing with the mouthpiece in a low position again.

A Gradual Change

When a student needs to change an aspect of his/her established playing habits, many teachers will simply tell the student to "play the new way from now on." This approach works well for simple things like altering hand position or taking a bigger breath, but for major changes involving the embouchure, oral cavity, or tongue, it works poorly. The student quickly finds it impossible to play as before and often becomes demoralized because s/he sounds like a beginner. The intense struggle involved in trying to change an established conditioned response while playing the instrument can also result in the development of new bad habits, such as excessive tension and forcing. This way of habit replacement usually takes a very long time.

The process of habit replacement using strangeness is truly superior in terms of ease and speed, and it is less stressful for both student and teacher. Teachers who use this technique may need some imagination to come up with a strange way to reinforce the new behavior away from the instrument. The student should be shown how to practice the new behavior and initially instructed to spend a small amount of time reinforcing it during each practice session. The student should be instructed to continue to play normally at all other times, such as in ensembles and performances. At some point, usually weeks (or possibly months, depending upon the strength of the habit being replaced), the new habit will become reflexive and automatic, just like the old habit. The student is now "on the fence," able to play using both the new and old behaviors, and it is time to make a choice. From this point onward the new behavior must be used exclusively and the old behavior halted completely.

An old Spanish proverb states, "That which grows slowly grows well," and this is certainly true of the process of habit replacement. At first the student spends a few minutes reinforcing the new behavior at each practice session, but as it starts to feel more familiar and comfortable, the time should be increased. If the student becomes overly fatigued, starts forcing, or has trouble playing his/her normal way, then the process is being rushed and the pace should be slowed. Close monitoring by the teacher is recommended since students often have a poor sense of proportion with regard to balance and moderation. I have had many students who insisted on trying to change their embouchure within a few days, even though I made it clear that they were to do only a few minutes per practice session over the course of a semester. Rushing the process usually results in problems.

Changing by Sensation

When we undertake a change of habit, the new behavior will feel awkward and wrong. It is natural to rely on this awkward sensation to tell us if we are playing the old way or the new way, but eventually the new way will begin to feel comfortable and familiar. The danger at this point is the unconscious tendency to start to exaggerate aspects of the new behavior to make it feel as awkward as it did initially. It is important to take into account the fact that time will change the sensations we are experiencing. To avoid this trap, rely on the sound, not sensation, as your guide.

Paralysis by Analysis

Making conscious changes to our technique requires attention to the physical aspects of performance. Too much attention, however, can result in a condition commonly known as "paralysis by analysis." It is characterized by a sense of confusion about the status and direction of the physical change one is attempting. Players experiencing this condition cannot stop mentally chewing on the details of the situation. They will usually obsess over choices, imagine negative future outcomes, and invariably try to consciously control processes that are largely unconscious, thereby turning the situation into a problem.

The greatest difficulty in working out deficiencies with technique is the task of keeping the attention focused on playing musically while at the same time remaining aware of the physical changes you are trying to reinforce. You must constantly remind yourself to play as musically as possible and to make a beautiful sound, especially on technical drills and exercises. When making changes in technique, know first what you want to sound like and work from that. Arnold Jacobs maintained that we must focus not on learning to play the trumpet but on learning to play music on the trumpet. To avoid paralysis by analysis, control the sound, not the body.

2

The Breath

Common Advice

There are more misconceptions about the breath than any single aspect of brass technique. Wrong ideas can easily have a detrimental impact on performance, and misinformation about breathing is still passed from teacher to student as it was a century ago.

Regarding breath support, it is not uncommon to hear teachers and performers exhorting us to "tighten your stomach muscles," "push your belly against your belt," "compress the air," and "support from the diaphragm". Legendary jazz trumpeter Dizzy Gillespie is credited with the most colorful admonitions: "Imagine you've got a quarter between your buttocks and don't make change," and "If the asshole ain't tight, you can't win the fight!"

Because much of this is generally accepted as correct advice, it may come as a shock that the single most destructive notion about breath control is the belief that we must tighten specific muscles in order to support the air column.

Arnold Jacobs

The principles that govern the control of the air in wind performance are widely known today thanks to the work of the late Arnold Jacobs, master pedagogue and former principal tuba of the Chicago Symphony. Jacobs studied wind respiration from a scientist's point of view and shared his research with students and colleagues. As his effectiveness as a problem-solver became known to the musical community, wind players from all over the world made a pilgrimage to his door. Jacobs never wrote a book about his work, but his revelations about the true nature of respiration and body use in wind performance have slowly trickled down, primarily through word of mouth, changing the older, misinformed views that brass players have held for decades. Even so, it is surprising how many brass players still believe in ideas that are counterproductive.

The respiratory system functions the same whether you are a great artist or a beginner. Misconceptions about the body cannot change the way that nature designed it to work, but they can make performing harder than it need be. Jacobs's contribution to brass pedagogy was to help us understand the most natural and efficient way to perform, allowing us to more easily discern the truth amid the differing theories, opinions, and conflicting schools of thought.

Although the world's greatest wind artists use the respiratory system in essentially the same way, it is not unusual to hear strikingly different accounts regarding how breath support is accomplished. Arnold Jacobs did not discover the correct way to play, but he gave us the language and concepts to understand what the body does when it is working efficiently, effectively, and in accordance with its natural function. For his contributions, generations of musicians owe him a great debt of thanks.

The Myth of Support

"I just tighten up my gut," says the trumpet soloist when asked by a student how to play high notes, and he punches his abdominal muscles to demonstrate how firm they are. Believing that mastery of the upper register can be accomplished exclusively by increasing abdominal strength, the student, with dedication and high hopes, begins his exercise campaign of daily sit-ups. Another frustrated trumpet player is born.

I was given similar advice in my youth from a band director who regularly hit his tightened abdominal wall with a fist while exhorting us in a strangled voice to "support!" Like so many young players, I believed that mediocre range and endurance on the trumpet were the result of a lack of strength, so I did hundreds of sit-ups, worked out with weights, and jogged for miles, but they did not help. There is no doubt that physical strength is extremely important in trumpet performance, but the average player is actually working much harder than necessary. For most players, the next step on the road to trumpet mastery involves doing less, not more. Increasing strength does not necessarily increase proficiency. Playing the trumpet is not purely a matter of power, but one of refining the coordination of many muscles to the point that we are using only those muscles necessary for the specific actions we perform.

Because brass and wind players contract the abdominal muscles (primarily the internal intercostals and obliques) when we exhale forcefully, it is natural to assume that consciously contracting them is the path to proper breath support, but this idea is based upon misconceptions about the workings of the respiratory system. The player who follows this advice will be fighting the natural laws of the body and activating an adversary that has shackled countless players to poor physical performance. That adversary is called the Valsalva maneuver.

The Valsalva Maneuver

Anton Maria Valsalva was an Italian anatomist who lived from 1666 to 1723. A celebrated researcher whose books continued to be used for many decades after his death, he was one of the very first to advocate the humanitarian treatment of the insane. He is also credited with the discovery that compression of the air in the thorax is accomplished by the contraction of the abdominal muscles and the sympathetic closing of the glottis. To experience this, clasp and lock your fingers together and try with all of your might to pull them apart. You will find that two things have happened: your abdominal muscles have tightened and your throat has closed.

The purpose of this function is basic and necessary: it is the primary mechanism used to push a newborn into the world, it allows us to remove bodily waste, it helps protect our internal organs from injury, and it is used to stabilize the spine and keep the core of the body firm during exertion. (Competition weight lifters are trained to consciously use the Valsalva maneuver.) When we tighten the abdominal muscles, the glottis closes sympathetically and keeps air from escaping from the body. The more the abdominals squeeze, the more tightly the throat closes.

Putting on the Brakes

In a misguided effort to "support the airstream," brass players unwittingly activate the Valsalva maneuver by overcontracting the abdominal muscles. With the Valsalva maneuver fully activated, very little air leaves the body despite the evidence of great exertion. The typical result is a bright red face, bulging eyes and neck, excessive forcing of the mouthpiece upon the embouchure, a strangled sound, and severely limited range and endurance. It is like driving a car with one foot on the accelerator and one foot on the brake: as the accelerator pedal is depressed, the brake pedal is depressed correspondingly. Likewise, when the Valsalva maneuver is activated, the throat only closes tighter as exertion increases. It is the epitome of inefficient trumpet performance. If this becomes the habitual way we play, high-level performance is not possible.

Grunting While Playing

The Valsalva maneuver is not an on-or-off proposition. It may be activated to a small degree. A sure sign of slight activation is the sound of grunting from the throat, similar to the sounds made when one is attempting to lift a heavy object. This occurs when the glottis is slightly closed and the vocal folds are excited to vibration. It is not unusual for players to be completely unaware that they are producing vocal noises while performing, but the sounds can easily be heard by plugging one ear. Though grunting while playing is a characteristic of Valsalva, not everyone who has activated it vocalizes when playing.

Just Blow

The solution to the Valsalva problem is simple: relax the abdominal muscles. How do we support the airstream with the abdominal wall relaxed? Some believe there is a secret technique to proper breath support, but nothing could be further from the truth. The simplest and most efficient way to create an airstream is by blowing. When we blow, the body automatically knows exactly how much to contract the abdominals. Without any conscious control or oversight, this task is accomplished with the fewest number of muscles and the least amount of energy. Most important, when we focus only on blowing, the throat stays open and the Valsalva maneuver is automatically bypassed.

Proving the Principle

Although heavy tension in the lower torso bottles the air in the body, a player who has been instructed in the old "tight gut" school of playing may find that idea difficult to accept. A demonstration may be in order to prove the point. Have the player blow as hard as possible through a small opening in the lips against a held piece of paper while consciously tightening the abdominal muscles. The paper will hardly move, as little air is leaving the body. Now have him/her completely relax the abdominal wall and blow freely through the same small opening. The paper will nearly fly from the hand.

Air Compression and Air Pressure

I remember arguing with one of my professors about breath support when I was a student at the University of North Texas. Don Little, professor of tuba and a former student of Arnold Jacobs, said that players confuse pressurization of air with movement of air, but they are not the same thing. I argued that trumpeters, unlike low brass players, must compress the air in order to play in the upper register, and that air pressurization is accomplished through firm abdominal muscles. It took time, but I eventually saw that Professor Little was right. As Arnold Jacobs put it, "Many people make the mistake of assuming that muscle contraction is what provides support. The blowing of the breath should be the support, not tension in the muscles of the body, but the movement of air that is required by the embouchure or reed" (Frederiksen 1996, 107). "With wind, there is always air pressure. With air pressure, there is not always wind" (Frederiksen, 119). In other words, to produce air pressure, don't worry about firming up the abdominals or any other muscle group—just blow.

Pressurized Air

Arnold Jacobs pointed out that the compression of the air within the thorax via the Valsalva maneuver is strong enough to cancel out the blowing mechanism. In his clinics, he would have a small person (sometimes his wife, Gizella) stand on the chest of a larger person lying on the ground holding his breath. This was to demonstrate that the musculature of the chest and abdomen, when Valsalva is activated, could easily support more than one hundred pounds. By contrast, we can only produce two to three pounds of air pressure when we blow as hard as possible. Therefore, tensing the abdominals in the mistaken belief that we are supporting the airstream actually traps compressed air within the body. When this happens, the free flow of air is slowed to a trickle or even stopped, and without air movement there is no sound.

The Relaxed State

There is another good reason for not excessively tightening specific muscle groups when we exhale. Sport science research has established that any physical task may be accomplished most efficiently when we start from a relaxed state. For example, try swinging a bat or golf club while your arms are tensed. You will find it difficult to generate any power or speed, and your technique will lack fluency and control. Now completely relax your arms and try again. There is no question that you can generate more power, speed, smoothness, and control from the swing that began from the relaxed state. The extra muscular tension that you added at the beginning of the swing actually robbed you of power. By the same principle, tightening your abdominals more than the amount required to blow freely is the same as adding tension to your arms while swinging a club; you will work harder, have less power and control, and run out of energy sooner. This "parasitic tension" can be found throughout the body, and it is the principal enemy of efficient performance. It can easily become habitual and is a difficult habit to break.

"Weakness Is Your Friend"

If tight abdominal muscles bottle the air in the body, does the abdominal wall remain completely relaxed when we blow? Muscular tension is necessary to create an airstream, so we can't eliminate all tension when we blow. (Blow vigorously and you will see that your abdominal muscles are firmly contracted.) To bypass the Valsalva maneuver, we must avoid the extra, unnecessary tension that is added to relaxed, free blowing. Arnold Jacobs specifically advised his students to make the abdominal wall "like jelly." "Tension in the abdominal wall is a trained response that is incorrect," he said. "Weakness in this region is your friend" (excerpts from Loren Parker's audiotapes). Jacobs was telling us to start the blow from the most relaxed state possible. When we activate the muscles of exhalation by giving the order to blow, the muscles will contract exactly as much as necessary to provide an airstream. I tend to avoid the word *support* in my teaching because it is so commonly associated with the excessive abdominal tension that activates the Valsalva maneuver.

The Sigh

A sigh requires no effort; it is the passive equalization of the air pressure between the outside air and the air in the lungs. The forceful exhalation used in wind playing is active; energy is required to create the air pressure necessary for performance. The primary difference between the passive and active types of exhalation is in the degree of energy used to expel the air, but they are fundamentally the same. Unfortunately, players often add extra, unnecessary tension when they blow more actively.

There are many different ideas and schools of thought about breath support, and it is easy to be confused. The simplest and most direct route to correct breathing is to relax and blow. If you have fallen into the habit of using excessive tension when you blow, the sigh can help teach you to breathe at a more relaxed level. Take in a full breath and let it out through a small opening in the lips. Do not blow; just relax and let the air go naturally without any effort. Do this several times before you pick up the instrument, and then begin playing softly at the same level of relaxation as the sigh. It will not be possible to remain completely relaxed when you begin playing with more power, but strive to keep returning to this relaxed state each time you inhale. With regular reinforcement of this relaxed state, you will find you are performing at a much more efficient level. It may seem to be a simple exercise, but the results are powerful.

A Blowing Exercise

One of the best exercises for strengthening the muscles of respiration is to blow against resistance. The instrument itself will work well for this purpose. Before starting your warm-up, blow three vigorous breaths directly into the lead pipe without the mouthpiece in the horn, and then blow three vigorous breaths with the mouthpiece in the horn. Without the mouthpiece, there is little resistance and you will find the air moving very quickly, but with the mouthpiece, the resistance is significantly increased and you will need to work much harder to move the same amount of breath. Try to keep the speed of the air constant through the blow, especially when it starts to slow as you get past the halfway point in the breath. Do not bend forward as you reach the end of the breath, but keep the body erect. Blowing firmly and freely to the end of the breath takes more physical effort with the added resistance of the mouthpiece, but this vigorous exercise will teach the body how to blow properly and efficiently. It is highly recommended as a pre-warm-up exercise or to energize your playing on days when things are just not working. (A more involved version of this exercise can be found in Irving Bush's *Artistic Trumpet Technique and Study* [1962].)

The Diaphragm

The lungs must contain air before a tone is possible, and it is the function of the diaphragm to draw air into the lungs. Inhalation is the diaphragm's only job; it has no part whatsoever in blowing air out of the body.

In its resting state, the diaphragm is a dome-shaped muscle that sits directly beneath the lungs at the bottom of the rib cage. The diaphragm stretches horizontally through the body from the sternum to the spine, dividing the thorax from the abdomen. Like all muscles in the body, the diaphragm can contract in only one direction, and when it contracts, it flattens. This action lowers the floor of the thoracic or chest cavity and increases its capacity. Other muscles also assist in the expansion of the chest cavity by pulling the ribs up and out, including the external intercostals, the scalenes, and the sternocleidomastoids.

When the thoracic cavity is enlarged via this muscular contraction, the resultant decrease in air pressure creates a vacuum that outside air rushes in to fill. Nature's natural abhorrence of a vacuum is the principle upon which inhalation occurs, and the diaphragm is its primary vehicle. The act of inhalation is similar to the action of a bellows or a syringe: the muscles of inspiration actively enlarge the thoracic cavity to create a low-pressure area that is quickly equalized by the air that is sucked in (Boyle's Law).

The idea that the diaphragm is somehow involved in exhalation is one of the most common misconceptions in wind pedagogy. While it is not particularly harmful to performance, I would love to see the phrase "support from the diaphragm" permanently out of circulation.

Just Suck

The diaphragm cannot be directly controlled; it is an involuntary muscle and only responds to commands from the brain via the phrenic nerve. When we wish to inhale, we cannot directly command the diaphragm to contract; we just order up an inhalation and the body takes care of the particulars. The specific way that we take the air into our bodies is a completely natural and instinctual act—we just suck it in. Inhalation is no more complicated than sucking, because that is exactly what it is. As stated by Arnold Jacobs, our goal is "maximum suction with minimal friction" (Brubeck 1991, 57). He suggested using the syllables "ah" or "oh" to initiate a relaxed inhalation, noting that we should feel the friction of the air at the lips, not in the throat. A noisy inhalation is the surest sign that there is friction or resistance in the body, usually in the throat. The path of the airstream must be free of friction.

There is no reason to actively raise the shoulders when we inhale, nor do we need to "expand" the back and sides. When we relax and inhale fully, the air naturally goes exactly where it needs to go. (After the abdominal region, the shoulders are the next most common place where performers tend to hold excessive tension.)

Haynie's Technique

John J. Haynie used a simple technique to demonstrate the proper way to inhale, which he characterized as "the breath of a drowning man." He would have a student jog for a few minutes and, upon his/her return, play a long tone. When the out-of-breath student finally gasped for air, it would always be a quick, full, and frictionless inhalation. After you have experienced this perfectly natural inhalation, there is never a question about what constitutes an efficient breath.

Breathing Through the Corners

With the mouthpiece on the embouchure, the proper way to take a breath on a high brass instrument is through the corners of the mouth or through the mouth slightly parted. It is necessary to breathe this way because there is often no time in the middle of a phrase to take the mouthpiece off of the embouchure, open the mouth, inhale deeply, and replace the mouthpiece. It is not proper technique to breathe through the nose. Young players who develop this habit must learn to breathe through the mouth corners, even if the teacher must resort to using a swimming nose plug to bring the point home.

The "catch" breath or quick gasp is used in situations where only a split second is available to take air in. This type of breath must be practiced like any other technique. In performance, there is a tendency to breathe in awkward places or run out of breath. Marking the places where you will breathe in the music will help to ensure consistency from performance to performance. This is especially important if catch breaths are to be used because they must be carefully planned.

The Lungs

The Science of Breath (1905) has been popular among brass players since the 1970s when top players like Bobby Shew and Maynard Ferguson regularly mentioned it in their clinics. In it, author Yogi Ramacharaka states that improper inhalation practices consist of three types: low breathing, mid breathing, and high breathing. In each of these types, he says, one only fills a localized portion of the lungs (35). Alan Hymes agrees, categorizing breathing into three types: diaphragmatic breathing, in which the chest cavity is expanded by the flattening of the diaphragm; thoracic or chest breathing, in which the muscles of the ribs expand the middle of the chest cavity; and clavicular breathing, in which the collarbones are raised to fill the top of the chest cavity (Hymes 1998, 30–32). Thoracic or chest breathing requires more effort than diaphragmatic breathing, and clavicular breathing is only used when the lungs are already relatively full and we wish to inhale to capacity. Diaphragmatic breathing, on the other hand, is the most efficient type of breathing; infants use it exclusively. Most people use some variation of either diaphragmatic or chest breathing in daily life.

Hymes notes that there is evidence linking thoracic breathing to a state of anxiety in the body and that chronic chest breathing might actually contribute to anxiety. In addition, he believes that since diaphragmatic breathing causes the lower abdomen to protrude, this may influence individuals on some level to use chest breathing since the modern body image model for both males and females dictates a small waist (37–40).

According to Yogi Ramacharaka, the "Yogi Complete Breath" is the preferred way to fill the lungs entirely. To accomplish this, you should "fill the lower part of the lungs . . . then fill the middle part of the lungs . . . then fill the higher potion of the lungs" (Ramacharaka, 40). In other words, you would employ diaphragmatic, thoracic, and clavicular breathing to completely full the lungs. However, Yogi Ramacharaka stresses that the Complete Breath is not to be done in three distinct movements, but in one continuous movement. The Complete Breath encourages relaxed abdominals and a deep, full inhalation.

Diaphragmatic Breathing

The primary difference between respiration on a musical instrument and our everyday breathing is in the degree of effort. In normal breathing, the purpose is to exchange oxygen for carbon dioxide. In brass respiration, it is to create wind pressure for the purpose of setting living tissue to vibration. Compared to normal breathing, brass players inhale larger amounts of air quickly and expel it with greater force. The function of the diaphragm is the exactly same in both types of breathing when a full breath is taken. (As noted earlier, however, it is possible to inhale without the use of the diaphragm, using chest breathing.)

The diaphragm requires absolutely no conscious monitoring or governing, and no improved way of functioning. It is a waste of time to think about controlling the diaphragm because it does not respond to conscious commands. The best advice is to leave it alone and let it do its job. A relaxed, full inhalation is the single most important thing we can do to improve the efficiency of wind instrument respiration.

The Abdomen

The movement of the diaphragm cannot be seen outwardly, but we can observe the effects of its action. When we inhale naturally, the viscera in the abdominal cavity are pushed down and forward when the diaphragm flattens. What many mistake for the movement of the diaphragm is actually the displacement of the internal organs when we take a big breath. It is extremely important that the abdominal muscles are completely relaxed when we inhale, for if they are tight, the internal organs will be held rigidly in the abdomen and the diaphragm will be unable to completely flatten. To demonstrate, tighten your abdominal muscles and try to take a deep breath; you will find that you can only inhale a partial breath. Now completely relax the abdominals and allow that region to expand outward as much as possible when you inhale; you will find you can inhale your biggest breath.

Abdominal Isometric

The brain automatically deactivates the diaphragm when we start exhaling, but it is possible for the diaphragm to remain in a contracted state when we employ heavy abdominal tension in place of proper blowing support. This creates an isometric muscular contraction between the diaphragm and the other muscles of respiration. Pitted against each other in a stalemate, these muscles only succeed in keeping the air bottled within the body. Hymes refers to this state as "paradoxical breathing," noting that it also occurs in the presence of strong emotions such as shock or rage (Hymes, 40–41). The way to avoid this undesirable condition is to remain completely relaxed at the moment of inhalation.

Relaxed Abdominals

The efficiency of the entire tone production mechanism is established the moment we take a breath. Any tension that has accumulated in the abdominal area during an incorrect inhalation will be transferred to the exhalation with predictably poor results. Tension can sneak into the inhalation when we are under stress, are fatigued, or are quickly grabbing breaths, such as in a piece of music where there is little rest or opportunity to breathe. The split second between the top of the inhalation and the moment we exhale is usually when excess tension slips in. Performing with too much tension in the abdomen is a difficult habit to break, but with patience and persistence, you will be rewarded with obvious gains in your performance ability.

If anything comes close to being a secret technique that has the potential to move your playing to a new level, it is this: always take a full, relaxed breath, and when you inhale, drop all tension from the abdominal region. This is harder than it sounds if you have been playing with excessive tension for years, but with practice it will yield a bigger, fuller, more focused tone, improved endurance, and an easier high register. The only way to prove it is to try it. I would suggest you start today.

Hara

Literally translated, the Japanese word "hara" means belly, but in practice it has a much greater meaning. Hara is the area located one to two inches below the navel and one to two inches within the body toward the spine. It is regarded as the body's seat of power by practitioners of zen and Asian martial arts, and a person is most balanced or centered when this point is the body's physical center of gravity. Many people believe the body's center of strength is within the upper body and shoulders, but in the martial arts, that belief results in an unbalanced and top-heavy posture that is weak and easy to defeat. Imagining that the breath is inhaled through the hara point is an excellent technique that can help establish the proper center of gravity and power. This is an important idea to experiment with in your practice.

Another Suggestion

Arnold Jacobs said, "Use your body at its tallest and longest with a relaxed frontal wall" and "Weakness in [the abdominal wall] is your friend" (excerpts from Loren Parker's audiotapes). I learned these points the hard way through trial and error over many years. One of the first exercises I invented to keep myself relaxed while playing was to imagine that my body from the waist down was completely relaxed, as if turned to lead or stone. By playing my practice sessions with half of my body absolutely relaxed, I found it easier to avoid excess tension throughout the rest of my body, especially during the moments that I habitually added excessive tension, such as when ascending into the upper register. When I did this exercise properly, I immediately noted the difference in my sound, and this convinced me I was on the right track. After much reinforcement it became automatic.

I have found at various times in my playing career that my old habit of using too much tension in the abdomen can gradually creep back into my playing. Even today, I make sure I am completely relaxed when I warm up. Vigilance during the warm-up is especially critical for those in the process of establishing new behavior.

More Reasons for a Full Breath

To perform with the least amount of effort, each inhalation must be full. When we take a full breath and let it out passively, such as when sighing, much of the air in the lungs is evacuated with virtually no effort. The moment the sigh naturally finishes is a stasis or equilibrium point where the pressure inside and outside the lungs is equalized. From this point on, it requires effort to exhale the remaining air in the lungs.

If you have to play a long phrase and you have taken a small breath in preparation, you will quickly reach the point of equilibrium, at which time you must actively work harder to blow out the remaining air in the lungs to finish the phrase. You would reach the equilibrium point sooner than if you had taken a big breath. Therefore, a full breath will require less energy to expel a given quantity of air than a small breath.

According to David Cugell, to generate the air pressure necessary to play a very loud, high note, our lungs must be completely full. He further states that there is only a limited period of time at the beginning of the blow when both the air volume and air pressure are sufficient to produce the loud, high note (Kelly 1987, 1006). This is yet another reason to take a full breath.

Vital Capacity

Our vital capacity, or the amount of air our lungs can hold, varies significantly from person to person and changes over our lifetime. Vital capacity can range from under two liters to over seven liters depending on your age, weight, height, and health, but some individuals are born with an unusually large capacity. Generally speaking, smaller people have less capacity than larger people and women have less than men. Athletes, wind instrumentalists, and others who use the respiratory system actively usually have greater relative capacity than those who are not active.

It is not unusual for a player to fall into the habit of taking in less than half of capacity when performing. As noted earlier, increasing the size of the breath has a very positive effect on performance ability, but Jacobs recommends against inflating the lungs to their absolute capacity, suggesting that 75 to 80 percent of capacity is a sufficiently large breath. More than this amount can create tension and inhibit the efficient exhalation of the breath.

Since our capacity decreases with age, we may gradually lose playing efficiency without being aware of it. One day, a player of advancing age may feel that things are not working properly in his/her playing. That day will come sooner if the player is in the habit of taking shallow breaths. Older players who have come back to the trumpet after many years are best advised do exercises to increase vital capacity.

Exercises to Increase Vital Capacity

Although our vital capacity steadily decreases from the peak of our late teens as we age, it is possible to increase it through exercise. Several excellent exercises can be found in Yogi Ramacharaka's *The Science of Breath,* but one of the best is to play long tones on the instrument. Inhale completely and hold a very soft note until the end of the breath. The note will shake or wobble as you reach the end, but by regularly practicing holding it past the point when the body habitually demands an inhalation, you can learn to increase your usable breath capacity. Holding soft and steady long tones until the end of the breath is one of the most basic and beneficial tone control exercises. It refines the entire tone production mechanism and improves response, control, finesse, and efficiency.

For all of these benefits from one exercise, it is a wonder that more players don't regularly play soft, long tones. Cat Anderson, the legendary lead trumpeter of Duke Ellington's band, played a pianissimo second-line G for twenty minutes every day. He claimed this "Twenty-minute G" was the secret of playing in the upper register, and many trumpeters paid cash to learn this secret from him. (See "The Twenty-Minute G" in chapter 5.)

Inhale to Capacity

Should we always inhale to 75 to 80 percent capacity, even for a very short phrase, or will a small breath do? In general, it is a good idea to get into the habit of always taking a full breath for the reasons mentioned earlier. Jacobs stated that there is no reason not to take a full breath.

Those who experiment with this idea find that they cannot deny the many benefits of a big breath—the results are convincing. Most players who experiment with inhaling more than their normal playing breath will instantly realize a larger, fuller tone, improved accuracy, and an easier upper register. It takes time learn to play this way. You will remind yourself a thousand times to take a larger breath than the one you are accustomed to taking, and after much repetition, it will become automatic. This is a technique that is virtually guaranteed to get results, but do not forget that if the inhalation is not free of tension, all benefits will be lost.

Circular Breathing

A technique called circular breathing makes it possible to give the illusion of an endless breath, but this technique has virtually no application in real musical situations. It is fairly easy to learn: while inhaling quickly through the nostrils, squirt out the air in the mouth with the cheeks and instantly return to normal blowing without a break or flaw in the tone. With practice it is possible to do this seamlessly, but the effort expended learning the technique may be better used elsewhere.

The Relaxed Throat

As noted earlier, when a player inhales and then tenses the abdominals, the Valsalva maneuver is activated and the throat closes, bottling the air in the thorax and causing the player to perform with excess tension.

Teachers commonly advise students to "open the throat" when the airstream is being choked off, but it is very difficult to open the throat while the Valsalva mechanism is activated. The simplest and most effective way to completely open the throat is to drop all tension at the moment of inhalation and stay as relaxed as possible when inhaling and blowing.

Years ago I had a student who was struggling with a closed throat that affected his sound and performing ability. I did not know the correct solution to this problem at that time, so I suggested that he work on "opening" his throat during his practice sessions that week. The next morning, I got a call from him. "You know that business we discussed about opening my throat?" he asked. "Is it supposed to hurt?" In the way that is so typical of earnest students, he was overexaggerating my suggestion to the point that he was hurting himself by trying to forcefully open his throat at the same time that his body was keeping it closed via the Valsalva maneuver. If he had relaxed his overly tensed abdominal muscles and just blown, his throat would have opened naturally.

The Glottis

The opening between the vocal folds in the larynx is called the glottis, and during a relaxed, deep inhalation, it automatically opens wide. We don't have to actively try to open the throat to inhale—our body will do this without any conscious direction. Efforts to open the throat wider will only introduce unnecessary tension into the inhalation. Players who believe they must consciously open the throat wider when they inhale often make an unusually loud or noisy inhalation or even a choking or gagging sound. In their efforts to open the throat, they are actually creating tension and closing the glottis to some degree.

Breathing doesn't have to be complicated. Sucking air into the body is one of the most natural things we do. However, taking a breath for the purpose of playing the trumpet requires a quicker inhalation speed and a greater quantity of air than our everyday breath. We have no need to open the throat; if we just suck the air in, the glottis will open naturally. As Arnold Jacobs said, "Start with suction at the mouth and let the air go where it wants" (excerpt from Loren Parker's audiotapes).

The Glottis as Valve

In *The Art of Brass Playing* (1962), Phillip Farkas discusses using the glottis in performance as a valve, claiming that the gross muscles of expiration are not capable of controlling dynamics with finesse and subtlety. He suggests slightly closing the glottis in order to produce a diminuendo, and to gradually open it from the semiclosed state to produce a crescendo (61). He reportedly regretted advocating this point after his book was published. The glottis, in fact, should not be used as a valve. We should not even have to think about the glottis when we play—it will do its job if we will just inhale and exhale freely. It is possible to control dynamics with great subtlety through the use of the muscles that blow the air out of the body.

Using x-ray photos, William Carter measured the glottis of twenty-four college brass students playing a loud high note, a soft high note, a loud low note, and a soft low note. His findings showed that the glottis size was larger for loud notes and smaller for softer notes, but it was unaffected by changes in pitch. Carter also measured the glottis of a flutist, whose instrument provides less resistance than a brass instrument, and he found once again that the glottis was larger only on loud notes. Carter (1996, 427) believed his data "support a theory describing the glottis as a semiautomatic aperture used to provide more resistance to aid the diaphragm and its related musculature in controlling the inward and upward contraction of the abdominal muscles upon exhalation." It is unlikely that Carter's hypothesis is correct. Aside from the fact that the diaphragm has no part in exhalation, the results he obtained more easily support the hypothesis that the internal pressure created by a large volume of wind meeting the resistance of the embouchure and the instrument (as when playing loud) is responsible for slightly enlarging the relaxed glottis. Enlargement of the throat, for example, is outwardly evident in players who are involved in strenuous performance, although when greatly exaggerated it may be a sign of a constricted throat or even a herniated neck. (See "Throat or Neck Hernia" in chapter 5.) Acting on Farkas's and Carter's advice that a player should consciously use the closing and opening of the glottis in brass performance is not recommended. The glottis's function is automatic, and it is best to let it do its job without interference.

Resistance

There are natural points of resistance within the body and in the instrument that are necessary for performance. When the throat is relaxed and the glottis is open as it should be, the first major point of resistance is the inside of the mouth or oral cavity. (See chapter 4.) Enlarging or diminishing the size of the oral cavity affects the airstream much like the thumb over the opening of a water hose, to use a common analogy. As the oral cavity is made smaller via the raising of the tongue and closing of the jaw, air pressure is increased, and as the oral cavity is made larger by the same mechanisms, the air pressure correspondingly decreases.

The next point of resistance is the embouchure. Air blown through the contracted muscles of the embouchure produces a vibrating air column in the instrument, and as the embouchure tension increases, the vibration frequency rises. The resistance in the oral cavity and embouchure constantly change depending on the needs of the music. This is done unconsciously through automatic processes that have been learned through repetition, and it is virtually impossible to consciously control these complex functions while making music.

There are two points of resistance outside of the body that remain fixed. They are the throat of the mouthpiece and the instrument itself. The mouthpiece throat is the smallest opening in the instrument, and like the instrument bore it is usually available in different sizes from the manufacturer. The player can also change the resistance of the mouthpiece by opening the throat with a drill. (I ruined many mouthpieces this way in my student years.) It is interesting to note that due to certain combinations of mouthpiece and instrument bore, a small-bore instrument can actually feel freer blowing than a large-bore instrument. For this reason, it is always best to try an instrument and not rely on a manufacturer's description of bore size.

Players unwittingly create points of resistance in their own bodies through excessive muscular tension, such as a closed throat caused by activation of the Valsalva maneuver. This tension can create a blockage that is blamed on the throat of the mouthpiece or the bore of the instrument. Excessive tension generally adds resistance to any task, reducing endurance and making it harder to perform. When we learn to relax and blow freely, unnecessary resistance in the body may be reduced or eliminated to a degree that we may be surprised to find how open the throat of the mouthpiece or instrument bore really is.

Suck and Blow

For many years I have been planning to make buttons to give out during my clinics. My wife has suggested it might not be a good idea to give young students buttons that say "Suck and Blow!" but with regard to wind respiration, there is nothing more to be said on the subject. The very heart of good wind playing starts by quickly sucking the air in and then freely blowing it out. It must be started from a completely relaxed state, and it must be automatic so that our attention is free to concentrate on making music.

Sucking and blowing comes naturally to everyone, but along the way some of us learn habits that lead to inefficiency and a host of common performance problems. It is ironic that a beginner with good breathing habits uses the air more efficiently than someone who has been playing incorrectly for years.

Warm-Up Exercises

The first warm-up period of your day should include a few moments to wake up the respiratory system to play. Often we approach the instrument at a low energy level, with our breathing shallow and our posture poor. Energize the breath by standing tall, inhaling fully and exhaling vigorously several times. Imagine the lungs as bellows and try to generate power and speed in your respiration. (Be aware of the possibility of dizziness.) In addition to waking up the body, this exercise reinforces the all-important habits of good performance posture, taking a full relaxed inhalation and blowing freely. (See also "Blowing Exercises" in this chapter and "Meeting the Effort Level of the Task" in chapter 5.)

Establishing Correct Habits

Players who have established a dysfunctional pattern of wind respiration are often unaware that it is the source of their performance problems. When they finally become convinced of this fact, the task remains to teach the body a better way. Altering unwanted patterns of behavior is not easy, but it is a necessary part of the work each of us must do to improve our performance ability.

New habits are established through trail and error, but there is a danger inherent in this process: trial and error can introduce new habits we don't want. For this reason, it is desirable to have a qualified teacher give you objective feedback on your progress and keep an eye out for potential problems.

Our natural inclination is to revert to our habitual ways of doing things, and these are extremely difficult to alter; we have spent many hours reinforcing the way we play, and our body will not learn a new way without a fight. Most players attempt to change unwanted habits while playing the instrument, but this is often a mistake as our learned behavior will interfere with the reinforcement of the new behavior. If you find it difficult or impossible to perform the new behavior with the instrument in your hands, put it down and practice without it. The key is to keep your attention on doing the new technique correctly over and over, regardless of whether the instrument is in your hands. Eventually your body will adopt the new behavior as habit and you will soon be able to perform the newly programmed actions while playing the instrument. (This process is discussed at length in chapter 1.)

A Practice Sequence

Doing the following sequence before your warm-up or practice session reinforces the basics of good respiration and will lead to improved playing habits.

1. Sit or stand tall with the abdominals completely relaxed, chest high without bending backward, and chin slightly in. Release the neck and shoulders and let the spine lengthen. Place the feet flat on the floor about shoulder width. If standing, unlock the knees.
2. Suck in a relaxed, full breath. Experiment with taking in more air than you are used to. Notice your posture when you are completely full.
3. At the top of your breath, while remaining as relaxed as possible, sigh through a small opening in the mouth. Do not force or try to work hard to do this—just let the air go and let it stop naturally. Do not allow your posture to sag; keep it the same as when full of air. Remain relaxed for a moment and go back to step 1.

Practice this sequence away from the instrument, such as while walking, driving the car, and while practicing fundamentals like long tones, scales, finger drills, and flexibility exercises. Repeat this sequence hundreds of times, and soon you will find yourself employing it (without thinking) in everything you play.

Refining the Sequence

When trying out new exercises or techniques, you may find through experimentation that a slightly different way of doing things produces a better result. If so, incorporate your new findings, letting the exercise change to accommodate your needs, and continue experimenting. Over the years, I have made dozens of minor discoveries that inevitably led to major breakthroughs in my playing. Through daily practice over weeks, months, and years, changes are slowly made. There are no shortcuts to the way we learn and refine complex psychomotor skill.

Conclusion

Excessive tension is the most common cause of dysfunctional breathing and the culprit for a variety of musicians' complaints. If we will focus our practice on making every breath completely free and relaxed during inhalation and exhalation, we can learn to play with ease. The results of unnecessary tension are clearly evident in the sound, and when it is gone, a large, rich, and ringing tone can be a pleasant shock. The real difficulty is not in convincing people of this idea, but in helping them to overcome this destructive practice after it has become a habit ingrained over many years.

3

The Embouchure

The Tone Production Mechanism

There are three components to the physical mechanism that produces a tone on a brass instrument: the embouchure, the oral cavity, and the airstream. Efficient performance lies in the balance and coordination of these three factors. When one or more of these elements is not doing its job correctly or sufficiently, the others will be called upon to pick up the load, resulting in poor form and bad performance habits. This imbalance is the primary reason for tone production problems.

The Embouchure

Embouchure is the word that wind instrumentalists use to describe the way the mouth is held during performance. It is derived from the French word *bouche*, meaning mouth. The definition of embouchure normally refers to the lips and facial muscles, but the teeth and jaw are integral to its function and the embouchure could not function without them. In addition, some players are unable to produce a buzz independent of the mouthpiece, so in such cases the mouthpiece itself might technically be considered a necessary part of the embouchure.

The embouchure is composed of approximately two dozen muscles of the mouth and face that collectively produce the tension necessary for vibration. Arnold Jacobs often described the brass player's embouchure as a "basket weave of muscles."

The primary purpose of the embouchure is to vibrate, for without vibration there is no sound. The embouchure does not make any sound until it is excited to vibration by the player's breath. Its function is fundamentally the same as the vocalist's larynx. Don Jacoby, renowned teacher and soloist, said, "The embouchure is just a reed."

Compared to the embouchure of a tubist or trombonist, the degree of tolerance for error in a trumpet embouchure is quite small. What may seem an insignificant change could have a profound effect. The embouchure is the trumpeter's favorite scapegoat, but it actually has less influence on performance than other factors such as excessive tension and poor breathing habits. William Adam, former professor at Indiana University, said "The embouchure is only 10% of trumpet playing, but it has to be 100% right."

Many tone production problems on brass instruments are not identifiable by sight because they are hidden under the mouthpiece or within the mouth, but an experienced teacher can identify problems aurally; the sound will always show where problems lie. A dysfunctional embouchure is among the most difficult problems to correct because it can be caused by so many different factors, including poor technique, incorrect placement of the mouthpiece, use of excessive force to produce compression, nerve or tissue injury, shape of lips, and configuration of the teeth. Embouchure function may also vary over time due to such factors as a change in practice habits, illness, and age.

Misconceptions about the Embouchure

One of the most widespread misconceptions about the embouchure is the myth of the "natural lip," or the belief that the embouchure is the sole reason for great performance ability. Spectacular high register and endurance, in particular, are cited as being the effect of "great chops," a phrase that has become part of the brass player's lexicon. Someone who is experiencing performance problems is said to have "lost his/her lip" even though the real cause may have nothing whatsoever to do with the embouchure. While it is true that most of the difficulties that occur during the careers of professional players are embouchure related, average players who struggle daily with chronic performance problems often have perfectly good embouchures. The root of their problems usually lies elsewhere.

The Brass Player's Face

A properly functioning embouchure has certain characteristics that may be found in virtually all properly functioning embouchures, but within general parameters there are infinite variations due to differences in physical makeup. Pictures of the embouchures of many of the world's finest brass players can be found in *Chops* (Spilka, 1990). Although there are predictable differences between individuals, there is a definite uniformity to the look of these embouchures. Phillip Farkas (1962, 19) characterized this look as "the brass player's face."

Occasionally we see a performer whose embouchure deviates significantly from the textbook model. An example is Dizzy Gillespie, who had a wonderful career in spite of, or perhaps to some degree because of, his herniated cheeks. No one can say whether he would have been a better trumpet player, physically speaking, if he had not developed this particular habit, but despite his personal success, this way of playing is not recommended as a good model.

The Message Controls the Mechanism

According to Arnold Jacobs, too much emphasis is placed on the look of the embouchure when we should focus on the sound and musical message we wish to communicate. He said that a fully functional embouchure is not formed by consciously trying to hold the face a certain way; it is formed over time by using it to make music. When we focus on music, the embouchure will gradually acquire the shape and function necessary to produce the sound we want without our conscious oversight or control. "Control the sound to control the meat. Think less of the muscle fibers and more like a great artist" (Frederiksen 1996, 123). A successful player's embouchure might be off center, asymmetrical, and unlike the textbook model, but that is generally of little importance if it functions effectively. If it works well, it is generally best to leave it alone. But what should be done if the embouchure does not function properly?

Conscious Control

The best way to replace bad performance habits with good ones is usually as simple as having the student imitate the teacher's sound, but this approach cannot solve all problems. There are times when we must consciously make changes to our technique based upon our knowledge of what is regarded as good form. If a student is playing with the inner rim of the mouthpiece on the red tissue or bunching the chin, for example, s/he must be made aware that these habits must be completely avoided and taught what to reinforce in his/her daily practice in order to correct the problem. Good musical images alone will not move the mouthpiece placement higher or flatten the chin. Diagnosing and prescribing a new pattern of behavior requires analysis of the problem and a conscious decision to make a change. On the other hand, too much analysis of the physical process is a common problem that can lead to "paralysis by analysis," a condition wherein the player has thought so much about the problem that s/he becomes confused by the many available choices and is unable to move forward (see "Paralysis by Analysis" in chapter 1.) A balance must be struck between the conscious and unconscious approaches when we are attempting to solve problems in the practice room. Ultimately, we must continually strive to produce the most beautiful and musical sound possible.

Automatic Function

The job of the embouchure is extremely complex. Its work cannot be audited or governed by the conscious mind, and it must function automatically to work properly. To understand the importance of automatic responses in high-level skill, imagine the difficulty of trying to regulate the exact degree of tension necessary to play successive sixteenth notes at a split second's notice. If a player needs to consciously control any part of the embouchure's job during performance, then there has not been enough practice to make that function automatic. Artistry suffers when our attention is focused on the physical aspects of making music. Our goal is an embouchure that is able, without any hindrance, to automatically respond to the musical messages from the brain.

Muscles and Nerves

The majority of the muscles of the face are gathered around the eyes, nose, and mouth since it is their job to control these orifices. These muscles are closely intertwined and generally work in groups. Although most of the muscles in the body are attached to bone on both ends, the facial muscles are attached on one end to the skull and on the other end to tissue, so that when they contract, the skin moves to accomplish the infinite variety of human expressions. Though various nerves serve the muscles of the face, the most important for wind players is the seventh cranial nerve since it controls the majority of the muscles of the embouchure. If this nerve is injured, it can have a devastating effect on performance. (See "Bell's Palsy" in chapter 5.)

The Pucker and the Smile

The brass player's embouchure is formed by two primary muscular contractions: the pucker and the smile. The conflict between these opposing forces produces the tension necessary for vibration.

The pucker aspect of the embouchure is accomplished exclusively by a single muscle, the obicularis oris. It encircles the mouth starting just outside of the vermillion (red) lip tissue. Although it is usually described as a sphincter muscle, it is not a true sphincter. The function of the obicularis oris is to close the mouth and to draw forward and protrude the lips. Farkas described it as having a "drawstring" effect (Farkas, 11).

Working in direct opposition to the puckering of the obicularis oris is a group of muscles in bilateral pairs that generally contract away from the mouth. Among the primary muscles of this "smile" group are the buccinators, which are located in the cheeks parallel to the upper rear molars. They extend from the jawbone and are attached directly to the obicularis oris at the corners of the mouth. The function of the buccinators is to pull back the mouth corners and firm the cheeks. They also control the sucking and expulsion of the air in the mouth—hence the nickname "the trumpeter's muscle." The risorius muscles, which are also attached directly to the corners of the mouth, are responsible for pulling the mouth backward into a leer or grimace. Other important muscles in this group include the depressor anguli oris, which pull the corners of the mouth down in a frown, and the depressor labii inferioris, which draw the lower lip down and flatten the chin. The group of muscles responsible for pulling the upper lip up and back include the zygomaticus major (elevates the mouth upward in a smile), zygomaticus minor (draws corners upward in a sneer), the levator labii superioris (elevates the upper lip), and the caninus or "snarl muscle." Muscles further from the mouth include the platysma, a muscle of the chin and neck whose function is to lower the jaw as well as retract and depress the mouth corners, and the masseters, the powerful muscles that close the jaws.

When all of these muscles are working together properly, the result is the firm, pursed look that is a characteristic of every successful brass player. It is of no particular use to know all of their names, but understanding their general function may be helpful in gaining an understanding of embouchure problems and solutions.

Isometric

The embouchure is an example of an isometric muscle contraction. An isometric occurs when two or more groups of muscles oppose one another to produce tension but not movement. An example is the vigorous pressing of one's palms together with equal intensity. Muscles shorten when they contract and lengthen when they relax, but in an isometric contraction, muscle length does not change significantly even though there may be a great deal of tension and energy expenditure. An isometric is static: the increase in tension in the opposing muscle groups does not produce motion because the muscles are in balance. Likewise, there is no movement at the corners of the mouth in a properly functioning embouchure. In other words, when a performer contracts or relaxes the embouchure when ascending or descending in range, the opposing muscle groups should increase or decrease their contraction in equal proportion. Just as our palms don't move in either direction when we push them together, the corners of the mouth should not move. If one of the opposing muscle groups is stronger, however, the embouchure will be seen to pucker or smile, and that generally means it is not functioning most efficiently and effectively.

The Smile Embouchure

A faulty embouchure type that was once taught and advocated even into the middle of the twentieth century is the so-called smile embouchure. It occurs when the muscle groups that pull back the corners of the mouth and flatten the cheeks, such as the risorius and buccinator, have won the isometric battle. As tension in the embouchure increases, the corners of the mouth move outward and sometimes upward in a smile.

There are several problems with this type of embouchure. In contrast to the thick, robust firmness of the normal contracted embouchure, the muscle tissue in the smile embouchure is stretched thin. The obicularis oris, in particular, is not allowed to firmly contract and is left vulnerable. The thinned lips are sandwiched between the teeth and mouthpiece and can offer only minimal resistance to the mouthpiece pressure necessary in performance. Flexibility suffers because this embouchure is easily pinned down, and the resulting decreased blood flow significantly lessens a player's endurance. In addition, the tone is typically small, thin, bright, and weak.

Smile embouchure players who are subjected to the demands of intense physical performance are prone to injury since they can quickly abuse the muscles and lip tissue of the embouchure. They tend to have more difficulty maintaining day-to-day consistency than those whose embouchure is a properly balanced isometric. They often complain of "swollen chops," and if they are in the habit of using excessive force, they may even find that they have tooth impressions or bleeding cuts from the sharp edges of the teeth pressed against the inside of the lips. The combination of a smile embouchure and excessive force can easily result in serious injury.

The Pucker Embouchure

The opposite of the smile embouchure, the "pucker embouchure," is less common. It occurs when the obicularis oris, the sphincter-like muscle that contracts toward the mouth, has won the isometric battle. The mouth is drawn forward in a pucker when this muscle is allowed to dominate, and flexibility, endurance, and range are limited. Response, especially at the softer dynamics, is poor. The tone quality is typically fluffy, tubby, and airy, and players who do not have a mature concept of sound sometimes confuse it with a "dark" tone. Pucker embouchure players will often find a normal, healthy tone too "bright" to their ear and resist change on the basis of this timbre preference. It may take some time for them to realize that their hollow, fuzzy tone lacks the focus and characteristic brilliance of a healthy trumpet sound.

The Bunched Chin

When the embouchure is working correctly, the chin should be flat, not bunched with the look of a peach pit. This is a common dysfunction, but it does not have as serious an effect on performance as other embouchure problems. To eliminate it, the student should spend several minutes a day away from the instrument just holding the embouchure firmly with the chin flat. When this can be done at will, the student should buzz simple tunes on this mouthpiece with the chin flat.

In time, the student can begin to play easy fundamentals on the instrument to gradually gain strength, and eventually the new position will become automatic.

Unorthodox Embouchures

Some teachers employ techniques that do not conform to the mainstream and accepted approaches to embouchure formation and tone production. In some cases they have produced students with extraordinary range using unorthodox techniques such as bunching the chin, exaggerated embouchure puckering, moving the lip aperture above the opening between the teeth, rolling the lips in or out, and jutting the chin forward to create an upstream set. That nearly all of the world's greatest players use what could be characterized as a conventional embouchure does not necessarily mean that alternative ways of playing have no merit. Most of these teachers enjoy a devoted and enthusiastic following, and I am among the first to agree that the most popular approach is not the best one for all. Common sense suggests that there must be a reason that the majority of players have not accepted such alternatives even though some have been around since the early part of the twentieth century. Deviating from time-proven and accepted techniques may mean sacrificing one parameter of performance in order to magnify another. Whether any of these approaches works is a question that each individual must answer for him/herself. Just as in the marketplace, caution is advised when considering any school or system that makes what seem to be outrageous or unrealistic claims.

Teaching the Embouchure to Beginners

Finding the proper balance between the embouchure's two opposing muscle groups is ultimately a matter of trial and error using both the proper "look" and a clear conception of the characteristic trumpet sound as guides. One technique that helps beginning brass players produce the right combination of pucker and smile is to have them try to whistle and smile at the same time. Another is to ask them to imagine tasting a lemon or smelling a bad odor, but without wrinkling their nose. Regardless of the technique used to reinforce the embouchure setting, the teacher should quickly move the student's attention to making a beautiful tone. Some beginners easily form the correct embouchure while others struggle just to produce a sound, even with the best instruction. If a beginning student cannot form the correct embouchure or produce a tone after a reasonable time, perhaps another instrument would be a better choice. Many players quit the trumpet in frustration after working day after day for years to acquire the simple performance skills that others take for granted. It takes more effort and dedication than the average person is usually willing to give to overcome chronic performance problems. In the majority of such cases I have seen, it would have been best if a teacher had suggested another instrument before too much time had been invested in the trumpet.

The Upper Lip Is the Vibrator

The results of a study done by Robert D. Weast (1963), former professor of trumpet at Drake University, show that that the upper lip is the primary vibrator and that vibration in the lower lip is in reaction to the upper lip. Using a mouthpiece of Plexiglas and a stroboscope disk, Weast observed that the upper lip (and the lower lip, to a lesser extent) was blown outward by the airstream. The elasticity of the tissue caused the upper lip to quickly return to its original position and bounce against the lower lip, repeating the sequence several times per second depending upon the speed of the lip vibration. Weast noted that the upper lip always went through the same sequence, but the movements of the lower lip were erratic: the lower lip tended to be more active in the lower register but became less active as the player ascended in range and the embouchure became firmer. In some cases, the lower lip had periods of no activity whatsoever, whereas the upper lip's activity was consistent in every one of the forty-two performers who participated in the study. Weast also noted that the lower lip was most active in subjects with even lip alignment, but subjects whose lips overlapped were more likely to have an inactive lower lip. Further, the amplitude or height of the aperture in the lips tended to be larger for loud or low notes and smaller for softer or higher notes.

The Aperture

One of the most misunderstood parts of the embouchure is the aperture, the opening in the lips through which the airstream flows. Some brass players mistakenly believe that they can consciously change its shape while they are playing and thereby affect tone color or other parameters of performance. (Farkas [1962]) devotes an entire chapter to this idea.) In fact, when the lips are placed together, the aperture is blown to its shape by the airstream. The aperture's shape cannot realistically be controlled by the player except by adopting an extremely exaggerated smile or pucker embouchure, or by opening or closing the jaw. These changes, however, will result in undesirable changes to the tone. As Farkas notes, the factors that determine the size and shape of the aperture include how firmly the lips are pressed together, how far apart the upper and lower teeth are, and the volume and velocity of the airstream itself. The critical balance between these factors is determined by the needs of the music and is completely automatic; we learn over time to gauge these parameters for the best results by using our ears. Attempting to take conscious control of aperture size may only result in excessive embouchure tension and unnecessary playing complications. Visualizing and striving for as focused, ringing, and resonant a sound as possible is the proven way to find the correct aperture size for any note.

Scar Tissue

Scar tissue along the buzzing surface of the lips can result in diminished or inconsistent response since this type of tissue is relatively inflexible and numb. It is a good idea to try to move the mouthpiece to a position that avoids scar tissue in the aperture area since tone production problems generally will not improve over time. It is possible for a player with a congenital defect or a healed facial injury to play a brass instrument as long as there is a place where the lips can buzz free of scar tissue and the muscles of the embouchure are not disabled.

Double Buzz

One supposition about players with a double buzz, characterized by a garglelike imperfection in the sound, is that an uneven lip surface is oscillating in two places at once within the aperture. Roger Sherman (1979) believes it occurs most often when the lip is fatigued and there is an uneven distribution of mouthpiece pressure on the upper and lower lips. He suggests changing the angle of the horn or jaw to equalize the pressure (21). Arnold Jacobs called a double buzz "segmentation," stating that the problem is caused by insufficient air to an embouchure that is too tight for the intended pitch and exacerbated by a tongue that is too high and forward within the oral cavity. He suggests relaxing the embouchure to buzz at the proper pitch and supporting the tone with a "thick airstream" (Frederiksen 1996, 126).

Many players find they have a double buzz after periods of heavy playing, particularly if they have been using excessive force. Usually this is a temporary condition that can be alleviated over a day or two through the use of soft long tones and easy lip slurs, or simply by taking a rest from the instrument. Players who have a permanent double buzz may find the only solution is to move the mouthpiece slightly to one side or the other to see if a clear buzz is possible with a new embouchure setting. One shouldn't worry about a little "dirt" in the sound; some of the world's greatest players have imperfections in their tone that are audible close to the bell but not to the audience. If this condition does not seriously affect a player's tone production, it may be best to leave it alone, but soft long tones combined with a good concept of the desired sound can often clear the tone over time.

Lip Compression

Lip strength is a critical factor in trumpet performance. A forceful airstream can easily overwhelm a weak embouchure, so the musculature of the embouchure must be capable of powerful compression, especially to produce the high frequencies at loud dynamics. A strong embouchure is mandatory for successful trumpet performance, and it is the direct product of playing the instrument regularly. Unfortunately, a dedicated practice regime does not always produce a strong embouchure; a lot of the wrong kind of practice is much worse than too little of the right kind. In addition, problems attributed to a weak embouchure are often the fault of poor posture, incorrect breathing habits, use of excessive mouthpiece pressure, and other causes.

Weak Embouchure

Virtually any healthy individual has the potential to develop a strong, fully functional embouchure. It is a myth that facial musculature strong enough for extraordinary range and endurance is a gift given only to a few. A lack of practice is the primary reason for "weak chops," which often results in the use of excessive force, poor breathing habits, and other problems. A weak embouchure causes an imbalance in the tone production mechanism: with the embouchure unable to carry its weight, the player must resort to excessive pressure to produce the necessary compression, and as the embouchure grows weaker and weaker, more and more force is used.

The No-Pressure Player

As a youth, I recall hearing older musicians talk about players of decades past who were capable of playing high notes on a trumpet or cornet suspended by a string. The truth is that the anemic sounds produced by an instrument played in this fashion are unacceptable for musical purposes. The so-called "pressureless" method of performance is a myth, although players of past generations touted it as an achievable goal for all serious performers. The pressure that all brass players must use to achieve a good seal between the embouchure and mouthpiece will normally increase when playing loudly and/or in the high register, and even the greatest players in the world use a bit of excess pressure at certain times. In correct performance, however, the muscles of the embouchure primarily produce the compression necessary for performance. Excessive mouthpiece pressure can be a temporary crutch used as a last resort, but if one is not careful, it can also become an insidious habit.

Compression by Force

Players can easily develop the bad habit of substituting excessive mouthpiece pressure for the proper use of the musculature of the embouchure. The use of excessive force is an extremely common brass performance problem that has kept thousands of brass players from achieving their musical potential. Ironically, forcing the mouthpiece against the embouchure actually does help one to play higher. Farkas gives an excellent analogy of what happens when we force the mouthpiece against the embouchure. He compares the embouchure, sandwiched between the teeth and mouthpiece, to a soft, spongy doughnut between two pieces of plate glass. As the plates of glass are pressed together, the doughnut is flattened and the hole in the doughnut gets smaller. Likewise, forcing the mouthpiece excessively against the soft lip tissue will compress the lips together, making the aperture smaller and high notes easier, but at a cost (Frakas 1962, 53).

It is impossible to determine the exact amount of pressure needed for normal performance or to know the exact moment when the muscles of the arms have taken over the job of the embouchure. A prominent red ring or deep indentation left on the embouchure by the mouthpiece can be a sign of the use of excessive pressure, as are rigid arms and a right little finger that is imprinted with a mark from the finger hook, but there are other, more obvious signs. When a performer who has been doing a lot of hard playing complains about a chronic loss of range, endurance, or flexibility, and when no amount of practice or rest can alleviate the problem, it is likely that the player has fallen into the habit of using excessive force. Another manifestation of excessive force is poor response, including notes that cannot be started at softer volumes and require a hard attack to get the lips to vibrate.

Even the finest players must use excessive mouthpiece pressure at times, such as when the embouchure is completely spent and the requirements of the moment demand compression that the embouchure cannot provide. It is easy to fall into the trap of using excessive pressure, but it must not be allowed to become habitual as it is a difficult habit to break.

There is a limit to the amount of effective pressure the embouchure can take before force begins to abuse the delicate tissues and musculature of the lips. Players who are in the habit of using force to generate compression will find that their range is limited; at some point, the lips simply can't be flattened any further and the aperture cannot be made any smaller. With no other alternative, the player using force will press the mouthpiece even harder in a vain attempt to get the notes to speak. Forcing the mouthpiece against the embouchure excessively for long periods can leave tooth impressions on the inside of the lips and temporarily loosen or move the teeth. Swelling of the lips is a common sign of this kind of abuse, but at its worst, excessive pressure can cause bruising, cuts, and even serious muscle and nerve injury to the embouchure. (See "Embouchure Injuries," "Nerve Compression," and "Muscle Tears" in chapter 5.) Megumi Kanda, who began her career by winning the principal trombone audition of the Milwaukee Symphony Orchestra, injured her embouchure using excessive pressure from too much practice as a student. If she had not learned to play without excessive pressure, her injuries could have ended her career (Nelson 2003, 21).

Chronic Embouchure Fatigue

Occasionally a student will approach me with complaints of poor performance, including decreased endurance, range, and response that seems to get progressively worse over a span of weeks. Usually the student has been working hard to prepare an important performance and has over-practiced and/or simply not afforded the body and embouchure any time for rest. A state of chronic fatigue is often the result of excessive forcing of the mouthpiece on the embouchure when we rely on it in ever increasing amounts to provide compression in place of the proper contraction of the embouchure. When this occurs, the only solution is to stop playing and let the embouchure recover. This is impractical for a working musician, but the player who has worked him/herself into such a predicament has little choice but to let the body heal. It is difficult to know exactly how long the healing process will take, but the player must resist the temptation to continue playing and risk making the situation worse.

Practicing to Collapse

A typical practice session for many dedicated young players involves practicing to the collapse of the embouchure. Although there is benefit in this approach, it requires careful rest and significant time away from the instrument in order to rebuild the embouchure after tearing it down so thoroughly. This type of practice also tends to reinforce the use of excessive force and can easily result in chronic forcing. In general, many short periods of practice throughout the day interspersed with rest is a much better strategy for building strength, developing healthy habits, and avoiding injury. Maurice André said that practicing in this fashion is the best way to develop endurance (Nelson and Alexander 1976, 733).

Rest as Much as You Play

Good practice habits are the major contributing factor in maintaining a healthy embouchure. One of the most time-honored rules of practice is to "rest as much as you play." Overuse problems would disappear completely if students would observe this simple rule. For example, if the mouthpiece has been on the embouchure for one minute, then the player should rest one minute before playing again. This allows the embouchure to recover much of its strength and resiliency. Bad habits are formed when a player has completely depleted the embouchure's strength but continues playing. Using the technique of resting as much as you play, you may find your practice sessions can last two or three times longer than usual.

David Baldwin, professor of trumpet at the University of Minnesota, took this principle a step further. Baldwin trained himself to quickly remove the mouthpiece pressure from the embouchure at every possible opportunity while performing, even during eighth rests. This technique allows the regular replenishing of oxygen and nutrients to the embouchure muscles that is critical to good endurance (Baldwin 1996, 58).

Resting as much as you play is one of the most beneficial pieces of advice I know. Following this rule allows us to practice for long periods without undue fatigue, avoids the possible reinforcement of bad habits that commonly occurs when we are overly tired, enhances and develops endurance in the long term, and builds strong embouchure muscles quickly.

Eliminating the Habit of Excessive Force

With regard to physical skill, we either move forward or backward, but we cannot stay in the same place. This is certainly true of players who habitually use excessive mouthpiece pressure since the embouchure will grow steadily weaker and even more dependent upon force when the arms gradually take over the embouchure's job of producing compression. Eventually the player will need a massive amount of force to play, and this will negatively impact every aspect of performance and put the player in danger of abuse and injury. This downward spiral will only get worse without intervention.

Eliminating the habitual use of force is a difficult, slow process requiring time and patience. Simply instructing the student to stop using force or to "pull the mouthpiece away from the face while playing" will not solve the problem as this habit is too deeply ingrained to be able to change consciously. Buzzing on the mouthpiece is an excellent diagnostic exercise to determine if one is using too much pressure. (For more, see "Mouthpiece Buzzing" in this chapter.) When alternating high and low pitches like a siren, it will become apparent that too much pressure is needed if the player has to grip the mouthpiece and forcefully press it to the lips to produce the higher frequencies. It is a convincing demonstration of the problem when these notes cannot be produced by any method other than force.

When done properly, mouthpiece buzzing is an effective way to eliminate the use of excessive pressure. James Stamp suggested holding the mouthpiece in the less dominant hand at the bottom of the shank with the forefinger and thumb. The other fingers should be splayed away from the mouthpiece and not allowed to curl inward as the need for pressure arises. As the player ascends, s/he will try to apply pressure, but the two-finger grip will allow only minimal pressure before the fingers start to slip up the mouthpiece shank. (In extreme cases, he suggested using the pinky or ring finger with the thumb as it is difficult to use any pressure this way.)

The body's call for excess pressure will usually come as the player ascends in range while doing exercises such as sirens, scales, and melodies. As this happens, the player should try experimenting with adding firmness to the embouchure, changing the oral cavity size as when whistling higher, and increasing the speed of the blow. Through continued experimentation with these factors, the proper balance will be found between the air, embouchure, and oral cavity size that will allow one to ascend using minimal mouthpiece pressure. The goal is to discover, using trial and error, a way to play that allows for the least amount of pressure with the greatest efficiency, playing effectiveness, and beauty of sound. The sound will always be your only guide: a clear, pure, focused buzz is a good indicator. On instrument, play with a soft, sweet singing sound. Playing loudly will only encourage excessive forcing and disrupt the balance one is seeking. This process takes time and patience, and it is critical that the player remain aware of the natural tendency to return to former unwanted habits.

Mouthpiece Buzzing

Buzzing the mouthpiece alone as a practice aid is a relatively recent phenomenon, and the use of the technique varies from player to player. When Maurice André, the great French virtuoso, first toured the United States in the early 1970s, he reportedly said that he had never practiced this way and was not aware of anyone who did. Max Schlossberg, in his *Daily Drills* (1938), recommended "a few notes daily." Renowned teacher James Stamp based much of his pedagogy on mouthpiece buzzing. Arnold Jacobs stressed this practice as valuable for connecting the ear to the embouchure and recommended simple songs and folk tunes in order to encourage musical expression.

There are many benefits to mouthpiece buzzing. Control, efficiency, and flexibility, among other things, are enhanced as the player strengthens the link between the musical brain and the tone production mechanism. As a player produces a more resonant and focused buzz, the sound on the instrument acquires these same characteristics. Pitch and accuracy are greatly enhanced when players realize the pitches they are buzzing are not the same as the pitches they wanted on the instrument. Buzzing a difficult passage and then playing the passage on the instrument can produce miraculous results. With only minutes a day over a period of time, it can also easily solve many tone production problems. Mouthpiece buzzing is an extremely effective practice technique that belongs in the repertoire of every player.

Jacobs had some of his mouthpieces cut away so that only a thin piece of the cup remained to connect the rim and shank, and he used these to practice mouthpiece buzzing while holding his tuba. There are commercially available devices, such as the BERP, which attach to the side of the leadpipe or fit into the leadpipe; these are essentially holders for the mouthpiece that allow one to mouthpiece buzz with the instrument in hand. The lip vibration is vented so it does not enter the instrument; the player holds and plays the instrument normally, but only the buzz is heard. Holding the mouthpiece between the thumb and forefinger will certainly suffice for buzzing practice, but combining the feel of the instrument and the manipulation of the valves will facilitate the transfer of the benefits of buzzing more quickly and directly to regular performance.

Most professional players today recommend mouthpiece buzzing. Many of them feel that mouthpiece buzzing is an essential part of trumpet practice and have developed specific and involved routines that they recommend to their students. James Stamp's *Warm-Ups + Studies* (1978), James Thompson's *The Buzzing Book* (2001), and the interactive DVD *Bert's Basic Brass* by Bert Truax, based on Stamp's ideas, are recommended. An instructional CD is also available from Mario Guarneri, manufacturer of the BERP and a former student of Stamp.

Although I highly recommend that every player experiment with mouthpiece buzzing, the amount of time spent mouthpiece buzzing, if any, is best determined on an individual basis.

Glissing

Among the best exercises for a player who is experiencing problems due to excessive pressure are soft flexibility drills, especially glissing, such as exercises 21 and 22 in Earl D. Irons's *Twenty-Seven Groups of Exercises for Cornet and Trumpet* (1938). The importance of playing extremely softly cannot be overstated: those who chronically play with excessive force will find it difficult to learn to play correctly when they play loudly since this approach tends to reinforce their problems. Soft playing allows you to discover the correct tone production mechanisms through a gentle trial-and-error approach. For example, try playing very soft glissing exercises while focusing on making a clear, singing sound. Keeping the body as relaxed as possible, especially the abdomen as Jacobs suggests, will prevent activation of the Valsalva maneuver. The gliss should be continuous without breaks in the sound, and under no circumstances should you use excessive force when you reach the point where range is difficult. Instead, experiment with air speed, tongue level, and embouchure with the sound as your guide. Through experimentation and repetition, you will discover the part of your playing that is out of balance. The sound you make will tell you if you are playing correctly; if the embouchure is contracted too tightly, for example, the sound will be stuffy and dull, but when all aspects of tone production are balanced, the sound is ringing and focused. It is imperative that the inhalation be relaxed and full. With persistence and patience, the proper way to play will be discovered. Over time, these notes will grow in strength and volume.

The best way to acquire the beautiful tone and quality of effortlessness that a fine performer demonstrates is to use such a person as a model. Hearing a master of the instrument play and taking that memory into the practice room is a proven route to success. I will never forget hearing Robert Nagel playing smooth and effortless three-octave glisses when I was an undergraduate student. It took some time, but I was eventually able to imitate him, and the memory of how he sounded guided me every step of the way.

Pedal Tones

Pedal tones are the notes below the normal range of the trumpet—that is, below low F-sharp on the B-flat trumpet. Many of the world's finest trumpet and cornet players have advocated their daily use. They are rarely used in musical situations because of their tone quality, but they are extremely beneficial for embouchure strength and range development. There are several suggested sets of fingerings for the pedal register, but I was taught to use the same fingerings as the notes an octave higher. (For an excellent discussion of pedal tones, as well as four different sets of fingerings, including those used by Herbert L. Clarke, see Olsen 1964.)

Pedal tones are not played with a loose or flabby embouchure, but rather with a more firmly contracted embouchure similar to that used in the upper register. For this reason, many players find that pedals are excellent training notes for the high range. An upward gliss from a pedal tone is usually easier than starting from a note in the normal low range because of the firmer embouchure setting of the pedal. The primary difference between the pedal register and the upper register is the size of the oral cavity, which is open for the pedals and closed for the upper register.

Pedal tones may be hard to play initially, but with practice they will come. According to James Stamp, blowing firmly and tilting the bell up slightly (for players with a downstream pivot) will sometimes help to produce the particularly difficult pedal C (one octave below middle C.) Pedals are especially beneficial as a warm-down after heavy playing because they quickly reestablish the balance between the airstream, embouchure, and oral cavity.

Pedal tones are among the most beneficial exercises I know, and I credit them with extending my range and endurance. Though they are highly recommended, I have occasionally encountered players who had difficulty playing them correctly and did not derive any benefit from them.

Embouchure Exercises

There are ways other than performance to strengthen the embouchure; some of the most common have circulated for so long that no one can claim authorship. Years ago I experimented with a smile/pucker exercise ("oo-ee"), as well as one that involved holding a pencil between my lips. I did not do them consistently and I was never really convinced that they were very helpful, but this impression may have been more a result of my haphazard application than from any lack of virtue from the exercises. It is also possible that any benefits may have passed my notice because the desired effect appeared days later and was attributed to something else.

One of the disadvantages of isometric exercises, which involve muscle contraction but not movement, is that strength is developed within a very limited range of motion (for example, pushing one's palms together). This is not a disadvantage for brass players because a brass player's embouchure is isometric in function and a properly functioning embouchure does not move when the muscles are contracted. Isometrics are ideal for exercising the embouchure because they employ the facial muscles in the same fashion as when we play our instruments.

Following this logic, it could be argued that the most effective embouchure exercise would consist of setting the face as if preparing to play and holding it firmly. It is the tension between opposing muscle groups that causes the resistance necessary for tone production, and these muscles are exercised when we systematically contract them. When holding the embouchure firmly, it is important that the facial setup be exactly the same as when we are playing and that the smile and the pucker muscle groups are balanced.

The greatest benefit is derived from this exercise when the embouchure is held firmly until the "burn" of fatigue is felt in the muscles, and then completely relaxed. The exercise may be repeated one or two more times, allowing a rest between each one. One session a day, or alternating days, has the effect of making the embouchure very strong, but these can be overdone. Getting enough rest to allow the muscle tissue to rebuild is every bit as important as the exercise itself. I have found it convenient to do this exercise when I am driving, working at the computer, watching a film, or reading. The best time is in the evening after the day's playing is over. If done in the morning, it may take a toll on the embouchure. For that reason, this exercise is not recommended when you are expecting to do a great deal of important performing. As with all things, moderation is advised.

There is some research that points to a six-second interval as being optimal for holding an isometric, as opposed to the "overload" type of exercise advocated here; you may wish to experiment with contracting for six seconds and relaxing for six until fatigued to see if this is more effective. As with any exercise, the amount of time it takes to get the "burn" becomes longer as you become stronger.

Some research indicates that using the same isometric exercise exclusively could lead to stagnation in strength in as little as six to eight weeks. One approach is to alternate isometric exercises with auksonic exercises (where both length and tension of the muscles change) such as the "oo-ee" exercise mentioned earlier.

Players who have dysfunctional embouchures or who play with excessive force will derive little benefit from isometrics, as additional strength will not solve their problems. This exercise is not a substitute for regular practice on the instrument, but rather an effective supplement. I have found that I am able to maintain excellent endurance with a minimum of practice when I do them every other day, but my accuracy and feel for the instrument suffers if I have not also been playing the trumpet regularly.

Lip Shape

The shape of the lip has the potential to adversely affect trumpet performance dramatically. For example, some individuals are born with an upper lip that has a rounded or pointed piece of flesh that dips downward or bulges in the middle. This bulge on the lip is called a *tubercle* or a "dew drop," and an upper lip with this distinctive shape is nicknamed a "Cupid's bow." Because of the potential trouble it can cause, it is reason enough to persuade a prospective trumpet student to choose another instrument.

The lips form an opening or aperture when they are blown apart by the airstream, but in the presence of the tubercle, the thickness of the tissue in the middle inhibits the formation of an aperture. This makes response difficult when normal lip compression and mouthpiece pressure are applied, and in the upper register where greater compression is needed to produce the higher frequencies, it is often impossible to even make a sound. When the dew drop overlaps the lower lip, it virtually ensures that when any pressure is applied with the mouthpiece, the aperture will be sealed shut.

Players cursed with this lip shape usually don't know it is the source of their performance difficulties. Frustration over their lack of consistency from day to day, even moment to moment, can cause them to make subtle adjustments to the way they play. Unconsciously, they will start to slightly part their lips when they set the mouthpiece on the embouchure in an attempt to reduce the tissue mass at the aperture area. This may lessen the problem to a degree, but inconsistent response, a stuffy or foggy sound, limited range, and poor flexibility are still to be expected. In addition, they will often move the mouthpiece to a lower position on the embouchure so that the inner edge of the mouthpiece is placed in the red tissue, a practice known as "playing on the red." This solution is no better than the problem it attempts to solve. (See "Playing on the Red of the Upper Lip" in this chapter.)

A characteristic of the player with a Cupid's bow lip is the often chapped quality of the tubercle. It is possible that this chapped condition is caused (or at least exacerbated) by the airstream as it is forced between lips that are unable to freely vibrate because of the mass of flesh at the aperture. These flakes of dead skin at the critically important aperture area make response even worse.

Fixing the Dew Drop Embouchure

There is a fix for the dew-drop lip embouchure, but it involves an embouchure change. The embouchure will not function properly with the mouthpiece placed in the middle of the mouth, but when it is placed to one side, there is a good chance that a player can perform normally after going through the arduous task of learning to play with the mouthpiece in a completely different spot. With the mouthpiece in the center of the

Cupid's bow lip, there is little chance that anything but frustration will result, even with superhuman determination and hard work.

Trial-and-error experimentation is the only way to find the best new placement for the mouthpiece. Usually one side will produce better results than the other. After determining the best position, the player should begin with simple exercises in the low register such as long tones, mouthpiece buzzing, and easy lip slurs. Very gradually, the player should introduce more complex lip slurs, chromatics, scales, and interval studies. Always insist on producing the best sound possible, even when it is difficult initially. Under no circumstances is the player ever to use excessive force to produce any note; if a note will not come except with force, then it is best to abandon it and try again in another practice session. With persistence and patience, the change has the potential to yield a normally functioning embouchure. (See "Changing the Embouchure" in this chapter.)

Mouthpiece Placement

There is some question about the placement of the mouthpiece with regard to the proportion of each lip in the cup of the mouthpiece. J. B. Arban (1936, 6) suggested "⅓ upper and ⅔ lower" in his *Complete Conservatory Method*, and this has been the accepted standard for generations of trumpet players. Arban also said, "There is no absolute rule for the position of the mouthpiece, for everything depends upon the formation of the mouth and the regularity of the teeth." The proportions of half-and-half and even slightly more upper lip than lower have been accepted in recent years because many fine trumpet artists play this way. For example, of the members of the Chicago Symphony trumpet section pictured in Farkas's *The Art of Brass Playing* (1962), two are using slightly less upper lip than lower, one is perfectly half and half, and one is using slightly more upper lip. I personally play with more upper lip in the cup. This proportion was not the result of a conscious decision; it simply evolved over time as the most natural and effective placement. For beginners, it is best to start with a mouthpiece placement that has been proven to work, such as one-third upper or half-and-half, but some players will automatically migrate to a position that works better for them. Extremely low or high placement, especially if it puts the inner edge of the cup in the red tissue of the upper lip, should not be allowed to occur as it will cause significant problems. (See "Playing On the Red of the Upper Lip" in this chapter.)

Off-Center Placement

Comfort and ease of response should determine where the mouthpiece is placed on the embouchure, whether centered or slightly to one side or another. In some cases players must learn to play significantly off center due to sharp teeth, a tubercle on the upper lip, or scar tissue that prevents them from playing in the center, which is the preferred position.

Although placement of the mouthpiece in the center of the mouth is preferable, off-center placement will not cause problems. Many fine professional players perform with the mouthpiece slightly to one side, and in some cases quite noticeably so. The teeth or lip configuration sometimes requires that the mouthpiece be moved away from the center; each player should be allowed to find the most comfortable and effective placement. Like water finding its level, the process of finding the best placement for the mouthpiece happens over time. A player may be unaware that the embouchure is off center until someone points it out.

When comfort, tone, and response are noticeably improved with the mouthpiece to the side, there is no wisdom in insisting that the embouchure be formed exactly in the center of the mouth. Some teachers believe placement should be visually perfect, in apparent disregard for the needs of the student. This misguided desire for symmetry may spell the start of a period of frustration for a player who may have experienced no troubles up until that point. In general, if center placement is the cause of tone production problems or unusual discomfort, then experimenting with moving the mouthpiece to one side is an excellent recourse. Use trial and error to let the body gradually and naturally find the best position with the musical end result as the guide.

Playing On the Red of the Upper Lip

To function properly, the inner edge of the mouthpiece must be placed on tissue that is supported by muscle, but the lips are composed of fatty tissue that by itself cannot support a normal embouchure. A performer whose mouthpiece inner edge is habitually placed on the red (vermillion) of the upper lip is using an embouchure that is not capable of producing the flexibility, strength, and endurance necessary for normal performance. It should be avoided at all costs.

The most obvious signature of an individual playing with the mouthpiece too low is the ring prominently inscribed in the red of the upper lip by the mouthpiece. In general, if this mark is any lower than the borderline between the lips and the surrounding skin, then the player is in trouble. An inability to play lip slurs (and the need to always tongue them) is another sure sign, as is a fuzzy, labored sound lacking a focused core, though sometimes the sound is quite good within a limited range, such as on the staff. Players with this condition often have very limited range; occasionally they are able to play high into the upper register, though they lack normal endurance, leaving them at a serious disadvantage. If an individual playing on the red has a large tubercle (dew drop) on the upper lip, s/he will usually have great difficulty producing notes above the staff.

A player usually adopts a bad habit such as this because s/he discovers that it produces certain positive results. Players who move the mouthpiece into the red may find initially that it helps range, and those with braces on their teeth find that putting the mouthpiece lower on the embouchure is more comfortable. Without proper feedback regarding the consequences of playing on the red, a player can easily adopt this way of playing without thinking about it.

Players with exceptionally full lips often have no choice but to place the mouthpiece on the red of the top and sometimes the bottom lip as well. In such cases, the solution is to have the player roll the lips in so that less red tissue is showing. This is not a small change and may require months of reinforcement, but it may be preferable to switching to an instrument with a larger mouthpiece, such as the trombone. (Armando Ghitalla, former principal trumpet of the Boston Symphony, discussed this idea in the November and December 1974 *Instrumentalist*.)

Sometimes a player—particularly big-lipped players—will place the mouthpiece in the red tissue of the lower lip, but this is generally not a problem as long as s/he is not playing on the red of the top lip as well. In an older style of French horn embouchure called *einsetzen*, or "setting in," the mouthpiece is placed into the fleshy red of the inner part of the lower lip. There are pictures of einsetzen in Farkas's *The Art of Brass Playing* (1962). This style of embouchure is no longer used or advocated by modern players.

The Double Embouchure

Some players perform on two different embouchures: one for the upper register and one for the low. Aspiring lead players, for example, may find that a particular mouthpiece setting gets better results in the upper register that their normal placement. This is not a desired technique because the player must reset the mouthpiece in order to cover the full range of the instrument, prohibiting the seamless movement from one register to another. According to Don Jacoby (1990), if both embouchures are relatively normal and functional, it is better to learn to play in the low register on the high register setting than to try to learn to play in the upper register on the low embouchure setting. He recommended playing everything on the high register embouchure and discarding the low register embouchure altogether. I went through this process when I worked with Jacoby one summer. Initially it was difficult to produce the notes below the staff without resorting to my low setting, but patient work with fundamentals such as scales and lip slurs produced a single embouchure capable of going from pedal tones to the upper register.

Slipping the Mouthpiece Down

Sometimes a player will gradually slip the mouthpiece lower and lower on the embouchure as s/he ascends in range, usually ending up playing on the red. The player must then take the mouthpiece off and reset it in order to play in the low register again. This problem, like other embouchure problems, takes great patience to correct. Using soft scales, mouthpiece, sirens, and lip slurs, the player must approach the "hot point," or the place where the mouthpiece starts to slip down. At the first sign that the mouthpiece is slipping, the player must carefully and softly reinforce playing in that part of the range without slipping down. Patient work over many weeks will gradually move the hot point up one note at a time until the player is able to play throughout the instrument's range without slipping. This same process works well to curb the use of excessive pressure.

Parting the Lips

The lips must be together (such as when saying the letter "m") at the commencement of the tone, but sometimes a player will fall into the habit of setting the lips slightly apart when the mouthpiece is placed on the embouchure. Most often this is because of an upper lip with a tubercle, as described earlier. (The following discussion applies only to players with a normal embouchure who are parting their lips. Players with a "Cupid's bow" lip should follow the procedure outlined in "Lip Shape.")

Playing with the lips slightly parted can result in an airy sound, poor response, and difficulty in playing softly. Correcting this embouchure fault is best accomplished away from the instrument. First, the player should spend a few moments buzzing the lips alone without the mouthpiece to get a sense of starting tones with the lips together, and then move to buzzing with mouthpiece alone. Be aware that when the mouthpiece is placed on the embouchure, the player will be compelled by unconscious habit to quickly part the lips the split second before starting the tone, such as when moistening the lips. It may be necessary initially to have the player say "m," place the mouthpiece on the lips, breathe through the nose, and then buzz without moving the setting or licking the lips.

The next step is to practice placing the mouthpiece on and off the embouchure while the lips are buzzing. This procedure does not give the player an opportunity to reinforce his/her normal mouthpiece placement ritual, including parting the lips. After hundreds of repetitions, a new habitual way of starting the tone will become automatic and the player will no longer have to think about placing the lips together.

Wet or Dry Lips?

Whether the embouchure should be wet or dry is a question whose answer will be determined by each player according to his/her needs, but the vast majority of players today perform with wet or slightly moist lips. "Dry lips" is a misnomer: the lips are not actually dry, just not lubricated by moisture. "Wet lips" means that the player licks or moistens the lips with the tongue, usually right before placing the mouthpiece on the embouchure. The advantage of wet or moist lips is that the embouchure is free to move when it is in contact with the smooth metal of the mouthpiece rim, allowing some flexibility in the placement of the mouthpiece. Dry players often use the stickiness of the mouthpiece against unlubricated lips to maintain a firm grip on the mouthpiece. In order to do this, they must keep the mouth and mouthpiece dry by wiping them with a handkerchief or coat sleeve. Renowned soloist and teacher Vince DiMartino, who plays dry, knows many professional performers who are very successful dry lip players. In some cases, however, with the leverage obtained from the lips stuck to the mouthpiece, some dry players are able to twist the mouthpiece in order to close the aperture and play high—a mechanical device that is a poor substitute for the proper contraction of the embouchure muscles. If sweat drips onto the embouchure and provides lubrication, the player will have difficulty playing. This method of generating embouchure compression is contrary to the established principles of good playing technique and can cause abrasions and sores due to increased friction on the unlubricated lips.

It is interesting to note that the subjects in John J. Haynie's videofluorographic study were instructed not to lick their lips because their tongues were coated with barium to be visible when X-rayed. (See chapter 4.) Haynie said he could not recall a single player who did not, or could not, start a tone without first licking the lips.

Changing the Embouchure

A dysfunctional embouchure prevents a player from being able to utilize all of the parameters of normal performance skill, such as flexibility, a beautiful characteristic tone, and reasonable range and endurance. Because of this, it is sometimes necessary to make changes to the way it functions. This is best done under the supervision of a qualified teacher and should not be undertaken lightly, as alterations to established performance habits can have unpredictable results. Though the actual fault may lie in another area of one's technique, the embouchure always seems to get more than its share of the blame for performance problems.

Both teacher and student should be aware from the outset that an embouchure change requires great patience, dedication, and perseverance in order to be successful. A student would be foolish to mount this task without a firm commitment to follow through and to trust the teacher's judgment. The teacher has a heavy responsibility to provide good counsel, feedback, and moral support when the going gets tough, as it inevitably will.

Changing by Sensation

One of the tendencies in changing habits such as an embouchure change is the over-reliance on sensation. Initially, for example, the new embouchure will feel strange and uncomfortable and the player will rely on this sensation to determine the position of the new embouchure. After the embouchure has been reinforced for some time, it will gradually start to feel more familiar, but the player will still try to seek out the strange sensation, and in doing so will inadvertently exaggerate certain aspects. For example, if the player is trying to move the mouthpiece higher on the embouchure, as familiarity sets in s/he will start to place it higher and higher in order to make it feel strange as it did initially.

The tendency to rely on initial sensations and to recreate them throws off the delicate balance that is being sought and leaves the player confused and unsure about his/her progress. We need to be aware that body feeling or sensation changes from day to day or even hour to hour, and sensation is not a reliable marker if used exclusively. Body sense (proprioceptive sense) or "feel" is vitally important in psychomotor skill, but it must be used in conjunction with close attention to the sounds we create with the instrument. The product we are seeking (music, sound) should receive our primary attention, especially when the new embouchure has begun to achieve a degree of independence and automaticity. Unfortunately, most young players learn the hard way that at some point in the embouchure change, they must take their attention off of remedial work (the physical side of the process) and put it on making music or they will find themselves quickly stuck in a rut, paralyzed by questions about whether they are doing the right thing. The answer is simple: focus on the sound that you want and trust your self to find the way.

Changing By Sight

It is extremely unwise to change a properly functioning embouchure just because it doesn't look like the textbook. Significant improvement is possible through certain alterations in the way we habitually perform, but changing a functional embouchure because of its appearance alone can lead a player into great trouble.

The folly of using a visual rather than aural guide for certain performance problems can be demonstrated with a true story. A successful freelance lead trumpet player approached me because he was having trouble playing. Someone told him he had "too much red showing" in his embouchure, and without questioning this advice, he set about changing his embouchure using a mirror as a guide. Within a short time, his playing had deteriorated, but his embouchure looked much better to him. Without explaining exactly what I was doing, I helped him reestablish his old embouchure using performance results as our guide. This player was so convinced that his embouchure had to have a certain look to be correct that he wouldn't believe that the old way was the better way. As inconceivable as it may sound, it is easy to fall into a similar trap when relying primarily on the eyes rather than the ears to make changes to performance skill.

Traditional Embouchure Change

The traditional way to change an embouchure is to instruct the student to play exclusively on the new embouchure and avoid playing on the old embouchure at all costs. This is difficult for a number of reasons. First, established habits will resist all attempts at erasure. Every time the mouthpiece is raised to the lips, the body will conform to the established patterns of behavior that years of repetition have made automatic and virtually immutable. Second, a player who has been asked to play only on the new embouchure will be unable to perform any better than a beginner for a period of weeks or quite likely months. This is difficult for a student in school ensembles and worse for a performer with professional responsibilities. The traditional approach is simply not the best way to teach the body new tricks. There is a better way.

Gradual Reinforcement

Rather than have a player sentenced to the purgatory of an unusable new embouchure, it is better to gradually introduce the new embouchure over a period of time while using the old embouchure for all performing commitments. For example, the player should spend a set amount of time during each practice session reinforcing the new embouchure through the use of low resistance fundamentals such as long tones and easy flexibility exercises. The more time one commits to the new embouchure, the quicker the change of habit, but if one intends to play well during the transition, some time must be spent practicing on the old embouchure as well. For all performance commitments, the old embouchure should be employed until the actual time of transition. Initially, it will be difficult to keep the old embouchure from reasserting itself during the period that the new embouchure is being reinforced. The new embouchure will feel unfamiliar and the player will unconsciously seek out the old embouchure. After a few weeks, the new embouchure will begin to feel comfortable, and though it will not be capable of handling the weight of normal performance, the player will be able to easily find and maintain the new embouchure position and configuration. Sometime after that, the player will be "on the fence," a condition in which the player can play on both embouchures or possibly find it difficult to play on either. At this point, the player must play only on the new embouchure and refrain from reinforcing the old one at all. The new embouchure will still be relatively undeveloped compared to the old one, but the player will have avoided the terrible period of poor performance that comes from using the new embouchure exclusively from the beginning of the change.

This approach to embouchure change may take a bit longer than the older method, but it is much less work for both teacher and student and better for the student's morale, and it builds a strong foundation to the new embouchure. The primary advantage, however, is that the student is able to separate the two embouchures and knows the location and feel of each, rather than the confusing and chaotic soup of sensations that usually accompanies the regular embouchure change. The first step is to have the student play for five to ten minutes per practice session initially; the length can be gradually increased according to the student's ability to sustain the new embouchure without resorting to force and excessive pressure. Typically, the determined student will try to speed up the process by practicing for much longer periods, but this should be discouraged. It is not possible for the body to learn any faster by force feeding, and it will surely cause the student to lose his/her balance, resulting in playing problems on both embouchures. Special care must be used during preparation for important performances since overemphasizing the new embouchure will usually adversely affect the performance of the old one. The key, as always, is moderation and careful attention to signals from the body. Most players are on the fence by the end of the academic term, and I instruct them to play exclusively on the new embouchure over the winter or summer break. From that point, it varies from player to player how long it will take before s/he is playing normally.

The gradual reinforcement method does make the embouchure change process easier and less prone to slipping back into bad habits. Because the player is able to use the old embouchure in rehearsals and performances, s/he is not placed in the position of having to use force to get through playing situations s/he wouldn't be able to handle on the new embouchure. Because this approach encourages relaxation and low resistance, it also reinforces efficient playing habits. (This is also discussed in "A Gradual Change" in chapter 1.)

A Final Word about Embouchures

It is foolhardy to unequivocally state what is correct or incorrect for any given player since a notable exception to any rule can usually be found. However, there are certain ways of forming and using the embouchure that are recognized as correct form, and there are ways that should generally be avoided. These determinations are not arbitrary, but are based upon generations of trial and error by our musical forbearers. Still, there exist degrees of correctness that defy the strict textbook definition, and it would be a serious mistake to change every little thing that looks wrong if the embouchure is working well. It is wise to approach an embouchure change with caution: there is an element of unpredictability inherent in the process, and sometimes a teacher's best intentions can go awry, leaving a student playing worse than before.

4

The Oral Cavity, Tongue, and Jaw

A View inside the Oral Cavity

"In the past," said John James Haynie, renowned trumpet pedagogue at the University of North Texas, "brass teachers had two basic methods of diagnosing student problems—they could listen to a student play and they could watch a student play" (Weeks 1968, 7). Brass teachers have always had questions about what happens inside the player's mouth during performance, and during the early 1960s Haynie took steps to answer those questions using the newest technology. Working with Alexander F. Finlay, a radiologist in Denton, Texas, Haynie used a fluoroscope and one of the earliest videotape recorders to document "jaw position, teeth and jaw aperture, tongue arching, pivot, mouthpiece pressure, position of tongue for attack, [and] position of tongue for double and triple tonguing" (Haynie 1968, 7). Although similar studies had been done earlier with Xrays by Jody Hall of the Conn Corporation, Joseph A. Meidt at the University of Iowa, and Fay Hanson at Weber State University, Haynie's study represented the first successful attempt to combine an image intensifier with a videotape recorder to produce moving X-rayed images with sound. Over a five-year period, beginning with still photography and moving to 16 mm film with a reel-to-reel audiotape that had to be manually synchronized with the movie, Haynie observed the performance technique of over seventy University of North Texas students and a number of professional performers, including Maurice André, Gerard Schwarz and the members of the American Brass Quintet, Richard Giangiulio (former principal of the Dallas Symphony), and big band leader Claude Gordon.

French trumpet virtuoso Maurice André was astounded: he was completely unaware that the tongue arched to produce changes in register. Like many of the world's finest players, he just did it without thinking. According to Haynie, few of the study participants had an opinion about the actions of their tongue and no one could describe exactly what happened inside the oral cavity. It is interesting to note that many of the poorer players improved by observing and imitating the action of the tongues of the finest players as demonstrated on the videotape.

Haynie's Results

With his subjects performing a variety of exercises in all registers, Haynie's observations included the following: virtually all of the subjects with a receding jaw thrust the jaw forward to align the upper and lower teeth; the vast majority lowered the jaw and brought it forward to play low notes; some subjects opened and closed the jaw aperture considerably more than others; all subjects arched the tongue during performance, which ranged from a quick snap into position to a smooth flowing motion; depending on the size of the tongue and oral cavity, which varied considerably, the tongue was seen to arch at the tip, middle, and back of the tongue; there was a more exaggerated arch for the soft and slurred arpeggio passages and less arch for loud and tongued arpeggios; virtually all subjects used some form of pivot (see "The Pivot" in this chapter), which included either a change in mouthpiece angle or a tilting of the head; each subject displayed the same pivot action whether slurring or tonguing; mouthpiece pressure increased when playing in the upper register and when playing at the louder dynamics; every subject used more mouthpiece pressure to prepare to play a high C than for the octave lower; during low register articulation, all subjects tongued between the teeth even to the point of touching the lips; when ascending into the upper register, the opening between the teeth got smaller and the tongue's position for articulation moved further back behind the upper teeth; the position of the jaw, teeth, and tongue was different when the syllables "tu" and "ku" were spoken aloud compared to the position used when the subject played them on the instrument.

The Use of Vocal Syllables

Singers describe oral cavity shape as it relates to spoken syllables, and this is the model that brass players have adopted. The most common syllables used to describe the change in the size and shape of the inside of the mouth on the trumpet are "ah" for low notes, "ay" for middle notes, and "ee" for high notes. ("Oo" has sometimes been used in place of "ay" for middle notes, but this syllable moves the tongue slightly back in the mouth, changing the timbre, and it requires a change in the formation of the lips.) Generally speaking, higher notes require a smaller oral cavity size and lower notes require a larger size. Each note requires a specific oral cavity size and shape, and any deviation from the optimum position will produce a less than satisfactory result. By analogy, a magnifying glass must be positioned carefully to amplify the sun's rays to produce the most heat. Similarly, any deviation from the most efficient oral cavity size will lead to a loss of focus and accuracy. Difficulties with range, both low and high, as well as accuracy and consistency of tone, can be traced to this basic part of the tone production mechanism. If a player is having a difficult time producing the notes in the low register, for example, a more open oral cavity, produced by an exaggerated "ah," will usually help, and players who are having problems with the upper register are often instructed to exaggerate the "ee" position of the tongue to make the oral cavity smaller. Tongue level is relative, meaning that an "ee" position at the top of the staff will not be the same as an "ee" position in the extreme upper register. The optimum position can only be found using experimentation, with the results as your guide.

While syllables provide an effective model for the correct oral cavity size and shape, the overriding consideration in tongue placement is the beauty and consistency of the tone quality in all registers. Too much focus on the syllables could be counterproductive if the attention is taken off of the quality of the sound.

Like Learning to Whistle

The process of learning to adjust the oral cavity size and shape for each note is exactly like learning to whistle. A child's early attempts to whistle lack accuracy, but with repeated trial-and-error practice, the technique of producing tones eventually becomes habitual and note accuracy increases. Gaining an understanding of the actual mechanism for changing notes is hardly ever a factor in the learning process; children just keep experimenting until they get the sound they want, never thinking about how it is done. The tongue, guided by the musical messages from the brain, automatically moves into the position needed for each pitch without conscious oversight. Like other aspects of trumpet technique, tongue movement is guided and determined by the ear; we simply hear the pitch and the body makes the necessary changes, like when whistling. We become increasingly adept at this through practice, and at some point the process becomes automatic.

Oral Cavity Size

As indicated by Haynie's results, oral cavity size differs from player to player, and this is an influential though invisible factor in performance ability. A player with a small oral cavity and large tongue, for example, would be more likely to have a naturally bright sound and possibly a good high register, and a student with a large oral cavity and a small tongue would be more likely to have a dark sound and an excellent low register.

In a story told by Reynold Schilke, Arnold Jacobs and a tubist from Japan were trying out a new tuba in front of an electronic tuner. After Jacobs played, the tubist from Japan found he had to pull the tuning slide considerably farther out than Jacobs to play in tune. Schilke was curious about why the same length instrument would not play in tune for both men. After some investigation, he determined that Jacobs's oral cavity was much larger than that of the Japanese tubist, and that the vibrating air column created by each player originated within the oral cavity at the back of the throat, rather than at the mouthpiece. In this case, the air column was longer for Jacobs due to his larger oral cavity and shorter for the Japanese tubist, and this required a change in the length of the instrument to match the tuner.

The Tongue

The tongue has an extremely important function in pitch formation since it is responsible for changing the oral cavity shape and size in conjunction with the jaw. Haynie's study showed that the part of the tongue that arches can vary from front, middle, or back based upon the size of the tongue and the oral cavity. Like oral cavity size, tongue size is a very influential determining factor in performance technique that can vary greatly from person to person (and over which we have no real control).

There are also striking differences between players with regard to tongue speed in articulation. (See "Tongue Speed" later in this chapter.)

In addition to changing the size of the oral cavity in conjunction with the jaw, the tongue is the mechanism that allows us to articulate sounds. (Of course, it is possible to start a tone using the breath alone.) The tongue acts as a valve; its action is generally down and/or back as it releases the air, but there can be great differences in technique from player to player.

Although we normally start the tone with consonants "T," "D" or "K," it is the vowel that determines the sound, so it is better to concentrate on the vowel, such as "tAH," "tAY," or "tEE," than on the attack. One suggestion is to think "T-Ha," with no separation between the "T" and "H."

Breath Attack

An attack with the breath alone is another style of attack that is available to a player, such as when an imperceptible entrance is desired, but it should not be employed as a replacement for the regular tongued attack. Instead of releasing the wind with the tongue, "h" or "p" is used to start the tone. Using breath attacks in practice has therapeutic value since the embouchure and oral cavity must be balanced and in the optimum shape or the breath attack will not speak immediately. Practicing soft breath attacks is one way to tell if one is forcing or if the tone production mechanism is out of balance, and soft breath attacks themselves are an excellent solution to the problem of poor response. Breath attacks promote movement of air upon articulation more than regular tongued attacks since it is possible to produce the consonant "t" without any movement of air, but "h" requires air movement.

Natural Tongue Placement

Arnold Jacobs characterized the tongue as "an unruly organ" that should not be given specific directions because it is difficult to control. As in all of his teaching, he advised players to focus their attention on the exact sound they wanted and the body would eventually find a way to produce that sound. In general, the tongue should be free to go where it needs to go to produce the desired sounds. Control of the tongue is best governed by the conceptual part of the brain.

One of the biggest revelations in Haynie's study was the confirmation that there is no single "correct" place to tongue. Depending upon the range of the notes in a given phrase, a player could conceivably tongue behind the upper teeth on the alveolar ridge (at the meeting of gum and teeth), behind the upper teeth, between the teeth, or behind the lower teeth. (The alveolar ridge is the bony prominence directly behind the upper teeth; the tongue touches it when we say "t," "d," "l," and "n.") The placement of the tongue during articulation is completely dependant upon the individual's physical characteristics and upon the tessitura of the note being played. In general, however, the tongue is placed higher (behind the teeth or on the alveolar ridge) for higher notes and lower (behind the lower teeth or even between the teeth) for lower notes. The exception is when the player uses the dorsal tonguing technique. (See "Dorsal Tonguing" in this chapter.) I generally avoid answering the question "Where does the tongue go?" because the answer varies from person to person and note to note. It is more important for the student to understand that when the sound and attack are correct, the tongue is in the right place.

Dorsal Tonguing

Herbert L. Clarke, the legendary cornet soloist and pedagogue, used a tonguing technique called dorsal or "anchor" tonguing as his primary method of articulation. Although this technique is not well known, some very fine players employ it. The technique involves keeping the tip of the tongue "anchored" behind the bottom teeth and tonguing with the middle or dorsal aspect of the tongue. (This is not the same as unanchored tonguing that produces the "th" articulated sound often used in jazz. See "Thick Tongue" in this chapter.)

In an article in the *International Trumpet Guild Journal,* New York trumpet artist and Juilliard professor Ray Mase discussed his use of anchor tonguing (Morton 2003). Mase stated that anchor tonguing provides an articulation with less "impact" that he finds attractive. In addition, he believes that dorsal tonguing is a more efficient mode of articulation since the tongue's movement is reduced, and that anchor tonguing puts the tongue in a more "natural" arched position. On these two latter points Mase hits upon the biggest advantages of dorsal tonguing.

Recently one of my students experimented with dorsal tonguing and determined it was not for him. The deciding factor was his inability to produce as precisely firm an attack as he obtained from conventional tonguing, which ironically is an aspect of dorsal tonguing that appeals to Mase. There is no particular reason for anyone to learn dorsal articulation if the way they were taught works well for them, but experimenting with it may prove to be of value to some players. Many players may be surprised to learn, however, that they use dorsal tonguing when they play in the extreme upper register.

Altissimo Articulation

It is difficult to keep the high tongue arch necessary for the extreme upper register when articulating with the tip of the tongue in the conventional manner. Because of this, many players actually use the middle part of the tongue against the roof of the mouth on the notes above high C. Some even anchor the tip of the tongue behind the bottom teeth, effectively dorsal tonguing, and are completely unaware that they have switched to a different technique. Articulating with the middle portion of the tongue as it is arched for the highest notes is a natural and easy way to tongue in the altissimo register. Those who use dorsal tonguing as their primary mode of articulation find it easier to articulate with consistency in all registers because they do not have to make a change in their tonguing technique when they change registers.

If a player uses a form of dorsal tonguing in the extreme upper register, there is often a noticeable difference in the articulated quality of the notes compared to the lower register. A player must be capable of performing all notes, regardless of tessitura, with the same consistency of articulation and sound. Two octave chromatic scales with the intent of producing exactly the same attack on each note are ideal for this purpose.

Spoken Syllables and Articulation

Haynie's study showed that there is a difference between the position of the tongue when articulation syllables were spoken and when they were played on the instrument. Because of this, he stressed that we should only use vocal syllables when teaching articulation to approximate the position of the tongue in the oral cavity and develop the proper concept, but we should not rely on syllables for the exact position of the tongue. Further, young students may inadvertently activate the vocal cords when articulating after they have heard their teacher speak the syllables aloud. When teaching articulation, it is best to demonstrate tonguing technique by tonguing and blowing and avoid making vocal sounds.

Tonguing between the Teeth and Lips

One of the time-honored rules of the early cornet players was to never tongue between the teeth, but the young Haynie found he did tongue between the teeth in the low register. As a teacher, he was disturbed that he endorsed a rule he himself did not observe, and this was the primary reason that he embarked on his study of the oral cavity. Through the study, he was gratified to find that fine players do tongue between the teeth in the lower register, and some may even lightly touch the lips with the tongue.

There is a lesson to all students here: what may work for one player may not necessarily work for another, and if an idea does not produce results after you have given it a fair trial, try something else.

Mode One

Most players use one style of articulation for general playing without thinking about it. This "default setting" can vary greatly in type and character from person to person and is partly determined by our personal preferences, our influences (especially our teachers), and our physical makeup, including the size and capacity of the tongue. It is a combination of the way we start the note (somewhere on the spectrum between a blunt and a sharp attack) and the relative note length (somewhere between full duration and very short). Determining a student's "mode one" is among the first things I learn about his/her technique.

Articulation General Tendencies

In general, those who use a very pointed or hard "t" style of attack tend to play everything very short, usually by stopping the tone early with the tongue, while those who play notes with a more legato or "d" style of attack tend to play notes full length. Players may be unaware of their personal articulation tendencies until they perform with others whose tendencies differ significantly from their own. Favoring one way of articulation for everything will not serve the music best, but ultimately we cannot escape the fact that each of us prefers certain sounds and approaches.

Having the widest possible palette of articulation styles to meet the needs of musical expression is the ideal, and it starts with the awareness of our general tendencies. If a student tends to play legato and long, it would be appropriate to assign studies in staccato and marcato, and if s/he tends to play "pecky," to choose study material with emphasis on legato. A student will have no difficulty maintaining his/her mode one for an entire etude but may have great difficulty playing an etude with an unfamiliar attack style and will unconsciously revert to mode one. Maintaining consistency of attack throughout the study will help the student to integrate new articulation styles and to expand his/her palette.

The ultimate goal for every well-rounded player is to be able to play comfortably and consistently with any style of articulation a situation calls for, whether notated in the music, asked for by a conductor, or required as a part of an ensemble or section. The ability to play with a wide palette of colors and styles is a hallmark of every fine professional player, and it is acquired through practice.

Combining Different Note Lengths and Attacks

Almost without exception, when I ask a student who naturally plays with a pecky "tut" style of attack to blow through and make full-length notes, the player will change to a legato attack without thinking. It is rare for a player to continue using a pointed or marcato attack when the notes are blown full length. On the other hand, when a student who tends to play long and legato is asked to play with a "t" attack, s/he will usually automatically shorten the note, stopping it early with the tongue by playing "tut." The repertoire often calls for full-length notes with a hard attack, such as in a fanfare, and it is just as inappropriate to use an extremely short note as it is to use a legato attack in such a situation. Combining different length notes with different attack styles must be practiced on the instrument like any other technique.

The Curse of Tut

The "tut" attack, or the abrupt stopping of the tone with the tongue, is used successfully in a variety of musical situations to produce an extremely short, hard, "dry" note, but it should not be confused with staccato. A staccato should have a light, bouncing effect similar to a string player's pizzicato. It can be represented visually by a bullet shape, with a clean, firm attack and a short body of tone that decays immediately. Staccato is created at slow to medium tempos through regulation of the air to produce little "puffs" of tone. The "tut" attack, on the other hand, consists primarily of an attack and abrupt cutoff, but very little tone.

Staccato

Staccato is often defined as short notes with space between them, but when we articulate quickly, we can no longer control the length of the notes or put space between them. At a fast tempo, the end of one note is the beginning of the next note, so ironically we are playing a form of "tut" attack. Therefore, what distinguishes staccato articulation from other articulation styles, particularly at faster tempos where we cannot control note length or the space between the notes, is the style of attack, usually characterized as a firm "T" attack.

Decay of Forward Motion

We have four available choices on every held note: to crescendo, to decrescendo, to hold the note at a constant dynamic, or to stop the sound. One of the most common interpretive faults related to articulation is the unconscious habit of playing every held note with a decrescendo or decay of energy. This tends to break phrases into small pieces and ruins melodic phrasing. A held note in the middle of a phrase is more likely to need a slight crescendo to continue the forward motion of the phrase, rather than a decrescendo, which halts the forward momentum. A related fault is the tendency to put breaks between notes in the phrase rather than blowing through and connecting the melody as a singer would. It is a common observation that students will interpret a phrase vocally with beautiful, connected phrasing but will play it on their instrument in a disconnected, unmusical style. Alternating phrases between the voice and the instrument is a valuable practice technique.

National and Historical Styles

With respect to the musical preferences and traditions of the world's many cultures and historical periods, we are often required to change our habitual approach to articulation, tone, and vibrato when performing music that is different from our own place and time. This requires knowledge of the style and sometimes techniques particular to a given nation or period. Some believe that the spoken language of a people might help us to gain a better understanding of their musical style, especially about articulation. This is an intriguing idea worthy of investigation.

Multiple Tonguing

Multiple tonguing is a technique that allows wind players to articulate much faster than conventional single tonguing. It involves substituting a "k" attack for a "t" attack every other note in double tonguing ("t-k," for example). In triple tonguing, the "k" can be played every third note ("t-t-k") or as a modified double tongue ("t-k-t"). Although most players use the "t-t-k" for triple tonguing, "t-k-t" is equally effective and may be easier for some players. I learned both styles of triple tonguing, and over the years I have found one to be better in certain situations than the other.

Woodwind players often use a "t-k-t, k-t-k" for triple tonguing, which is just a double-tongue figure fitted into a triplet pattern. This technique is uncommon among brass players and not generally recommended because every other triplet group starts with a "k" rather than a "t" articulation, which can result in an audibly weaker or different attack when the "k" is employed. Without a great deal of work to ensure that the "k" sounds exactly like a "t," this style can produce less than consistent results.

As the speed of multiple tonguing increases, the "t" and "k" attacks tend to change into "d" and "g" attacks, and this is both normal and desirable. Playing with a sharp or heavy attack at the faster speeds will slow the tongue down. Although some definition of the attack is lost when we play with the more blunted "d" and "g" attacks, this is usually not an issue when tonguing very rapidly because it is too fast to be noticed.

Producing the "K" Attack

Learning to produce the "k" and making it sound exactly like a "t" attack is the first difficulty that must be overcome in learning to multiple tongue. The "k" does not have the explosive quality of the "t" attack (though this is less of a concern when the tempo increases and both attacks become more legato). Initially, however, it is important to exaggerate the explosive quality of the "k" in practice to make them sound equal.

The stroke of the tongue as it moves back and forth in the oral cavity during multiple tonguing should be as short as possible by bringing the "k" farther forward in the mouth. A shorter tongue stroke has the potential to significantly increase tonguing speed. Cornet soloist and instrument manufacturer Vincent Bach advised the use of "ti-ki" for all double-tonguing because "ki" is more forward in the mouth, whereas "tu-ku," as suggested by Arban, puts the "k" too far back into the throat. (It should be noted however, that the French pronunciation of "tu-ku" places the tongue farther forward in the mouth than the American pronunciation.) Using one syllable for multiple tonguing in all registers conflicts with the idea of different oral cavity sizes relative to register, but this technique seems to work well for many players.

Rhythm, Time, and Wind

Students typically attempt to increase the speed of their multiple tongue before they have perfected their technique. The result is a multiple tongue figure with an imperfect rhythm. Ideally, all double- or triple-tongued notes should be of equal length and exactly the same distance from one another, like a picket fence. Students will inadvertently get into the habit of playing figures that are not equal, such as a triplet that is played like two sixteenth notes and an eighth note, or a double tongue that is played like a sixteenth and a dotted eighth. The student is usually unable to hear these imperfect figures until they are slowed down. Insisting on perfect rhythm from the beginning will prevent the student from having to go back and relearn the technique. Students who practice articulating as rapidly as they can will also tend to vary the tempo according to the difficulty of the music they are playing, so a metronome should always be used to ensure perfect tempo.

Failing to blow though articulated figures results in another common problem: an attack with little tone following it. I sometimes compare the tongue to the cork ball in a referee's whistle, which cannot move without air to motivate it. Although the tongue is not blown around in the mouth, this image helps free the tongue and gets the air moving. Blowing steadily though articulated figures can usually improve multiple tonguing immediately.

An excellent multiple-tongue exercise is the two-octave chromatic found in Haynie's *How to Play High Notes, Low Notes, and All Those In Between* (1988). The metronome should be set at a tempo that allows the player to comfortably tongue a sextuplet (six notes) to each beat of the metronome—usually somewhere between sixty and eighty beats per minute. The object is to play the two-octave chromatic up and down alternately using single tongue, double tongue, and two forms of triple tongue without any noticeable change in the articulation style or rhythm.

To add difficulty and benefit, the player can try to play them all in one breath and, when that is possible, to add a slurred scale. Some may consider this to be a nearly impossible task, but Haynie could play this entire exercise with all four forms of articulation as well as slurred, twice through in one breath.

To summarize, students should focus on multiple-tongued figures that have perfect rhythm, a "k" articulation that sounds exactly like a "t," are played in perfect time, and are blown through and connected by the airstream.

Multiple Tonguing in the Upper and Lower Registers

Young players first learn to multiple tongue the notes on the staff, rarely entering into the upper or lower registers in their practice. Many of them assume that if you can tongue well on the staff, then you can tongue well in all registers, but this is false. Tonguing in the extreme upper and lower register is so different from playing on the staff that it should be practiced as a separate technique. The Haynie two-octave multiple-tonguing exercise described earlier is perfect for reinforcing evenness, consistency of sound, and uniformity of articulation style in all registers. Listen carefully to be sure that there is no garbage or extraneous sound between the notes. Be sure the sound is always your best, as if each little note is cut from the cloth of your finest long tone.

Tongue Speed

Some players are born with an unusually slow tongue, and in most cases there is little that can be done to significantly increase the speed. A common myth about wind articulation is the "mother tongue" theory, which holds that tongue speed is related to the language speed of one's ancestors. According to this theory, a person of Spanish or Italian descent would have a quick tongue and a person of German or Slavic descent would have a slow tongue. This idea has been proven completely false, yet it persists. The reality is that some players are just born with faster or slower tonguing ability.

A player who has a slow single tongue can usually substitute multiple tonguing in place of the single tongue at faster tempos. To employ this technique, the double and triple tongue must be practiced slowly to be absolutely undetectable when used in place of the single tongue. This technique has worked for many players who struggle with a slow single tongue.

Articulation Problems

Some of the problems that affect articulation may be inherited, such as an unusually slow tongue, but most are acquired habits. As mentioned earlier, when working through articulation problems it is best to concentrate on the sound one desires rather than attempting to direct the tongue to specific actions or positions. When players are using poor articulation technique, it is not possible to see inside the oral cavity, so we must rely on the sounds they make to tell if there is a problem. Identifying some of these problems is difficult, even for an experienced teacher, but others are quite obvious.

Stutter Attack

Imagine that you are unable to start the tone after taking a breath, as if a lock has been placed on your tongue. Because of the similarity of this condition to a vocal stutterer's difficulty starting speech, it has been called a stutter attack. Individuals with this affliction are frustrated by the inability to start a tone except in a few circumstances, such as when a downbeat is given or upon the notes following an initial attack. Because an individual with this condition is able to tongue normally under some circumstances and not others, it is considered a mental rather than physical problem. Although this condition is quite common, even affecting some top professional players, little has been written about it.

Martin F. Schwartz (1991) has found that the vocal cords of individuals who vocally stutter are pressed together so tightly that the air pressure that normally sets the vocal cords into vibration cannot pass through. He believes this is a learned behavior that results from the struggle to speak, and the real cause is anxiety and stress. All of the players I have known that developed the stutter attack condition did so without any discernable physical cause, but many expressed the belief that a fear of making an error upon the attack precipitated the problem.

A common treatment for spoken stuttering is to speak in rhythm, and while this may produce an unnatural robotic effect for a speaker, it is a good strategy for sufferers of musical stuttering. Most players with this problem have no difficulty starting a note to a conductor's downbeat, so one treatment for the stutter attack is to tap the foot to the beat of the music for a bar or so, inhale in time, and attack the note. This has been an effective solution for most of the stutter attack sufferers with whom I have worked, but it must be practiced constantly until starting the tone this way is automatic. It is not uncommon for a relapse of the stutter problem to occur when a player assumes this problem is fixed and discontinues practicing breathing and tonguing in tempo.

Schwartz noted that the individuals he studied who had recovered from a speech stutter tended to precede their first word with a barely audible sigh. Its purpose is to allow the vocal chords to relax, unlocking the voice box and allowing speech to occur. If this were applied to wind players suffering from a stutter attack, the player would take a breath, release a little air as a sigh to unlock the respiration apparatus, and then attack the note. At this writing I have not had the opportunity to try this technique with a stutter attack sufferer, but it sounds promising. The key is patient and slow work to train the body to automatically remain relaxed at the moment that the tone is started. After this has been established, Schwartz believes it is important to drop the habit of thinking about the stutter at every potentially difficult situation, which could trigger the problem again. This is not easy to do, but it is essential to success that the player believe that s/he is cured and can play normally again. Without the eventual establishment of absolute confidence that the attack will occur when it is needed, the problem could reoccur at any time.

Thick Tongue

Some players articulate with the flat part of the tongue (the blade or dorsal aspect of the tongue) instead of the tip, which produces a "th" quality. Unlike dorsal tonguing, the tongue is not anchored behind the bottom teeth. Jazz musicians often use this attack style (Harry James and Clifford Brown were two of many who used it), and it is perfectly appropriate in that musical context, but it is not a good choice for the classical player who must conform to established norms of sound and style. Articulation is one of the most important identifying characteristics of a musical style.

Chew Tonguing

Any movement by the jaw during articulation will be apparent in the sound. The most common problem of this kind is a quick and minute lowering of the jaw at the moment of articulation that produces a "twa" attack. Sometimes called false crescendos or chew tonguing, this flaw in the technique of young brass students usually goes away after the player has been made aware of it and begins imitating good models, but in extreme cases a more direct approach may be necessary.

I had a student who jerked his chin downward exaggeratedly with each articulation, yet when he articulated without the trumpet, he had no jaw movement whatsoever. As soon as the mouthpiece touched his face, however, he began chewing again. I had him practice tonguing and blowing (without buzzing) with the mouthpiece almost touching his face, and eventually he was able to touch the mouthpiece lightly to his embouchure and tongue without any jaw movement. The next step was to add the buzz to produce a tone on the mouthpiece alone, and only when he was successful did he work with the instrument. It took more than two weeks of patient effort on his part, but he was finally able to tongue normally on the instrument.

The Teeth

The embouchure is based upon and supported by the teeth. If the teeth are absent, have sharp edges, are of a very uneven configuration, or have a severe malocclusion such as an exaggerated under- or overbite, there is a good chance of performance problems, even if the musculature of the embouchure functions perfectly. Changing the shape of the teeth, particularly after one has been playing for a number of years, can have drastic and unpredictable results and should not be undertaken lightly.

Brass players are particularly susceptible to performance problems involving the teeth. A list of famous jazz trumpeters who had dental problems that adversely affected their careers includes Louis Armstrong's mentor Joe "King" Oliver, Bunk Johnson, Bobby Hackett, Buck Clayton, Bill Coleman, and Chet Baker. The legendary Bix Beiderbecke had a removable front tooth that fitted over a tooth broken during childhood. This dental prosthesis was loose and had tendency to fall out; on several occasions it left Beiderbecke completely unable to play until it was found (Spencer 2002).

A Tooth Crisis

Someone once said that every serious player will have at least one embouchure crisis in his/her life. I have had my share, including one involving the teeth. A small bump developed on my lower lip in the middle of the aperture that prevented me from playing any note above second-line

G on the staff. This bump was placed exactly on the lower lip opposite a protruding tooth. I tried every suggestion that came my way, but this problem would not go away. I started taking a real estate course because I believed my music career was over. On the advice of my teacher, I engaged the assistance of a dentist, who made me a retainer that slowly altered the shape of my teeth, allowing me to adjust gradually. The bump soon disappeared, and after four of the darkest months of my life I was able to play again. (A lesson with James Stamp during this period was another important factor in my recovery.)

Years later, a student with sharp front teeth developed a similar bump on his lip. I suggested he see a dentist, but he resisted the idea. A local physician advised him to have the bump surgically removed, and against my advice he had the procedure done. When the bump reappeared a short time later, he left school still unable to play. I believe that he would have solved his problem had he consulted a dentist or orthodontist.

Although changing the shape of the teeth can solve certain problems, you should exhaust all reasonable recourse before making changes. It would be wise to seek the advice of the best players in your area to obtain the name of a dentist who is sensitive to the needs of brass players or knowledgeable about your particular problem. In general, take small steps and be patient; to try to rush this kind of change may ultimately cost you dearly.

Optimal Teeth Formations

Few brass teachers have detailed knowledge of the various types of teeth configurations and their effect on performance, and precious little has been written on the subject. Perhaps the first and most comprehensive research was done by Matthew and Edwin Shiner, professors at Duquesne University, originally published in the *Tri-State Digest* in 1961. The Shiners maintained that the optimal upper (maxillary) teeth formation must have a convex contact point or "V" where the mouthpiece is placed. This configuration is the most effective for performance because the "V" bears the weight of mouthpiece pressure and supports the embouchure, yet it allows free vibration of the embouchure on either side of the contact point. A natural curve to the line of the upper teeth with the central incisors at the point of the "V" is ideal, but any tooth protrusion or overlap near the center of the mouth can serve as the contact point. (The embouchure does not need to be perfectly centered to function properly.) If the contact point is too sharp, it will cause other problems, such as discomfort, pain, or even cuts. The worst formation is a convex or completely flat tooth surface, which has the effect of pinning the embouchure down and inhibiting a free and ringing tone when even minimal pressure is applied.

Bill Pfund, former professor of trumpet at the University of Colorado in Greely, expanded upon the work of the Shiners. The diagrams in his book, *The Trumpeter's Pedagogical Guide* (1992), detail several of the best and worst maxillary (upper) and mandibular (lower) teeth formations for high brass instruments. In the case of irregularities and malocclusion, Pfund advises players to locate the position that best facilitates performance through trial and error, which could include moving the jaw forward, back, or even laterally. In cases where there is not a contact point or protrusion to allow optimal lip vibration, he advises considering orthodontics, but only as a last resort. Pfund suggests that teacher and parents first evaluate the student's potential and commitment to determine if the time and expense of such a procedure are justified.

Diagnosing Teeth Problems

Problems related to the configuration of the teeth are difficult to diagnose since few teachers and players are aware of the causes. I once had a student who could usually make a good sound on the staff, but his tone quality in the upper register was nearly always choked, strained, and unresponsive. After trying many possible solutions with no success, I took a careful look at his teeth and noted that the two front incisors were angled inward, like an M. The high points of his upper tooth profile presented two usable V points on either side of his incisors at the canines, but he had been placing his mouthpiece between the two high points, at a place where the teeth offered no support to the embouchure. When he added even moderate pressure, the embouchure was pinned down and unable to move.

Moving the mouthpiece to the left or right so that the mouthpiece was centered over the V of the canines did not work well for him, so we used some dental wax (available at any pharmacy) to build up the two front teeth. In one short session of experimentation, he made a wax prosthesis that largely cleared his poor tone and eliminated his upper range problems. Though he needed time to get used to playing with the new shape of his upper teeth, the problem was effectively solved. The experimentation with the wax proved that the shape of his upper teeth had been the problem all along. Unfortunately, the soft wax tended to change shape from the pressure of playing and he found it necessary to take it out and reshape it constantly. A more permanent solution needed to be found.

Dental Appliances

Many fine wind and brass players wear devices in their mouths to overcome the limitations of less-than-optimal teeth formations. A dental overlay, for example, is a removable hard shell that fits over the player's teeth to achieve the best possible teeth configuration. This alternative to orthodontics has several advantages, including ease of placement and removal, easy adjustment to quickly determine best effectiveness, and the proven potential to completely correct a wide range of problematic teeth formations. Players who invest the time and effort to adjust to an appliance may find significant improvements in flexibility, range, endurance, and tone quality.

Finding a dentist who has experience helping musicians should not be difficult since dentists today are more conscious of the needs of musicians and most receive some instruction in these problems as part of their medical training. Unfortunately, many music educators are not aware of either the potential problems brass players can encounter with their teeth or the available solutions.

Dental Bonding

Ned Gardner (1996) was struggling with a painful protruding tooth that adversely affected his performance. He tried using dental wax to fill in the receded areas on either side of the offending tooth to make a more stable surface and noted a significant improvement in comfort, range, endurance, and sound. The dental wax was inconvenient to apply, as well as impermanent, and orthodontics was too drastic and time-consuming. The process of dental bonding was a perfect solution, as it was easy and fast to apply, reversible, and completely customizable. It involves the application of a plastic compound that is bonded to the teeth. When Gardner wrote about the procedure, he had been playing on teeth that had been bonded for three years and he was completely happy with the results. This is another excellent solution worthy of serious consideration. A qualified dentist can fully explain the procedure.

Braces

A period of adjustment is needed for wind and brass instrumentalists who have new orthodontic braces or those who have them removed. It is a toss-up which is more difficult—learning to play with new braces or relearning to play after they have been removed. In most cases it is a matter of one to two weeks before one is able to play normally again. Moderation in performance and plenty of rest between sessions will help speed the adjustment process.

For years, players have had to resort to orthodontic wax or rubber appliances to pad the brace ligatures and obtain relief from the pain of sharp edges, but those days may be over. Recent advances in orthodontia have yielded braces with ligatures on the inside of the teeth, as well as transparent plastic retainers that can be easily removed.

I have seen so many former brace wearers playing with the mouthpiece too low on the embouchure (with the inner edge on the red tissue) that I believe braces might often be responsible. It is possible that players gradually slip the mouthpiece down on the embouchure for comfort, and when the braces finally come off the bad habit remains. For this reason, I advise keeping a close eye on the embouchure placement of students who wear braces.

Wisdom Teeth Extraction

The extraction of the third molars, or wisdom teeth, is a common rite of passage between the ages of seventeen and twenty-two. They are often extracted because they are impacted within the gums or even the bone of the jaw. The amount of time necessary to heal varies depending on the number of teeth extracted and the difficulty of the surgery. It is important to find a good surgeon since complications from a poor extraction can have a negative impact on one's performance for a long period of time. One of the most serious concerns is the possible damage to the mandibular nerve, which would cause numbness in the lower jaw, lip, and tongue. If the tooth under consideration for extraction is near this nerve, one should weigh carefully the possible ramifications and obtain a second opinion. (For more information, see Mortenson 1990.)

The Jaw and Instrument Angle

The jaw's primary function is to close and open the oral cavity to provide the appropriate size to resonate for each note, as well as to provide the base of support for the embouchure. The jaw is also responsible for the angle of the instrument. If the jaw recedes, the instrument will point downward, and if the player has a pronounced underbite, the instrument will be parallel to the ground or even point upward. This angle dictates the direction of airstream as it enters the cup of the mouthpiece.

Some believe that the trumpet must be held parallel to the floor when performing, but comfort and ease of response should determine the best angle for each player. Marching bands and drum corps usually insist on instrument angle uniformity, which can cause havoc with a player's performance technique. One young man with an overbite learned to play with his head jutted forward and his chin up in order to align his instrument with the others in his section. This was contrary to all the laws of efficient body use and put his throat in jeopardy of a hernia when he played in the upper register. When he overcame these poor performance habits, his natural instrument angle was a much more comfortable downward angle, and every aspect of his trumpet playing improved dramatically. If the angle of the instrument is important, have a repair person bend the shank of the mouthpiece so that you do not have to make adjustments to your posture or embouchure placement.

Parallel Teeth

In his *High Notes, Low Notes, and All Those In Between* (1986), Haynie writes, "The ultimate range a person achieves is largely determined by the discretion used in allowing the lower jaw to recede." In other words, range becomes more limited to the degree that we allow our lower jaw to move inward, or recede, particularly when ascending in range. (Haynie was referring to the player with a downstream pivot; the opposite would be true for the upstream player. See "The Pivot.") The player who allows the lower jaw to recede as the jaw closes may find the upper teeth making contact with the bottom lip on or near the buzzing surface, and this can inhibit the lip vibration. Farkas (1962) also stated that it is desirable to have the upper and lower teeth parallel, but it should be noted that there are many fine players whose teeth are not exactly parallel.

Bringing the Jaw Forward

A player who is unhappy with range or tone production may benefit through experimentation with bringing the lower jaw forward so that the teeth are parallel. I myself made this adjustment. The process began when I noticed that I was able to produce a very high pitch when I buzzed with the lips alone with my jaw more forward than normal. I began practicing buzzing this way in the car and walking to class, and after a week or two I was able to produce very high, small notes on the instrument. It took a long time before I was able to perform with this new embouchure without my jaw receding, but when I could, my range had improved significantly. I eventually ended up playing with my teeth parallel in all registers, and I have played that way ever since.

Trumpet teacher William N. Costello in the 1930s was among the first to suggest to his students that high range could be more easily attained by jutting the jaw past the upper teeth, anchoring the mouthpiece to the bottom lip, and directing the airstream upward, effectively turning the student into an upstream player. (See "The Pivot.") Conversion to an upstream set in order to realize the extreme upper register has worked for many, but it is not for everyone. Players with a weak or receded chin sometimes find it difficult to keep the jaw forward for extended periods, and irritation of the jaw joint, including TMD, can result. (See "TMD and TMJ" in chapter 5.)

The Pivot

A change in the angle of the instrument as a consequence of the jaw moving forward or receding is called a *pivot,* a term coined by Donald S. Reinhardt. There is a good deal of confusion about whether the pivot is a part of good technique. Some believe that we should not move the instrument when we play, while others believe a pivot occurs naturally and should be left alone.

In fact, most players use a bit of pivot when they play but are completely unaware of it. For the vast majority of players, the instrument angles downward to some degree when it is placed upon the embouchure. This angle can vary significantly from player to player and is dependent upon the degree to which the jaw is receded when it is closed. Players who find that the instrument angles increasingly downward as they ascend and angles upward as they descend are called "downstream players." There is a small percentage of players whose instrument naturally angles upward when ascending and downward when descending due to the presence of an underbite. This is the reverse of the downstream player, so they are called "upstream players." There is evidence that players naturally play one way or the other, and while we may change the instrument's angle by bringing the jaw forward or back, it is not feasible or even desirable to turn an upstream player into a downstream player when neither has a distinct advantage.

Experimenting with the pivot can bring some benefit. For example, a downstream player who angles the bell of the horn angle slightly upward while descending to the low register may find that the low notes speak better and have more clarity and resonance. Too much angle can have the opposite effect, so trial and error with the sound as your guide is the only way to find the best position.

A pivot may also be lateral. A teacher once pointed out that as I ascended in range, I pulled the instrument downward and to the left. It was such a subtle movement that I was not aware of it, but it was clearly a part of the way I naturally played. I am grateful that my teacher did not try to change this aspect of my performance, since eliminating it could have caused me great difficulties.

Reinhardt's *The Augmented Encyclopedia of the Pivot System* (1973) made a science of the angle and conformation of the jaw and teeth. He devised an elaborate classification system that identified four primary embouchure types and several subtypes, each with a particular pivot. For a period of time, Reinhardt worked with many of the finest brass players in the United States, and his New York teaching studio was completely booked. With Reinhardt gone and only a handful of teachers carrying on his teachings, his influence on brass pedagogy is over. (For more information see Dudgeon 2000.)

Even Mouthpiece Pressure

There is another benefit to bringing the jaw forward to make the teeth parallel: the mouthpiece pressure is made even on the top and bottom lips or lessened on the top lip. Research has shown that the top lip is the primary vibrator, and transferring excessive upper lip pressure to the lower lip can have a positive effect on tone quality and endurance (Weast 1963). The upstream player, whose jaw is thrust past the upper teeth when ascending in range, is especially prone to exaggerated top lip pressure because that particular embouchure set makes upper lip pressure more likely. Excessive top lip pressure can make the tone thin, limit flexibility, and significantly reduce endurance. Experimenting with resting the mouthpiece primarily on the lower lip—"anchoring" it to the teeth of the jaw—could have very positive benefits for some players.

Vibrato

Vibrato is a subtle fluctuation of the tone that is used for expressive purposes. This fluctuation has two aspects: amplitude, which refers to how wide the vibrato is, and frequency, or how fast it is. Vibrato is ideally learned unconsciously from listening to master musicians and imitating them. There are two types of vibrato used by the American school of trumpet players: the hand or wrist vibrato, which consists of moving the right hand forward and back upon the valves to produce a wavering of the tone, and jaw or chin vibrato, which consists of a subtle chewing motion of the jaw. There is a third type, the breath impulse vibrato, which is sometimes known as diaphragm vibrato though it has nothing to do with the diaphragm. It consists of a "ha-ha-ha" breath-pulsing technique and is rarely used by American brass players today. (Through his videofluoroscopic study, Haynie discovered one fine professional trombonist producing vibrato with the movement of his tongue. It is difficult to tell how many individuals use this technique since it is invisible to the eye, but Haynie discovered only one case in over seventy players.)

The hand vibrato was more popular in the early to middle part of the twentieth century when virtuosos like Harry James and Rafael Méndez employed it, but the jaw vibrato is more common today. Some individuals believe that once the jaw vibrato becomes habitual, it cannot be turned off, and others believe that the chewing motion of the jaw interferes with tone production, but both ideas are false.

It takes time for some students to become accustomed to the use of this expressive device, but others quickly pick it up by ear, unaware that they are using it. It may be necessary to ask a student who is experimenting with vibrato for the first time to exaggerate it as s/he will tend to use it so subtly that it is almost undetectable. This is because the vibrato sounds overdone and even ridiculous to one who is used to a straight tone. Although it should ultimately become an automatic part of musical expression, vibrato can be practiced and refined like any other technique. Have the student put the metronome at MM=60 and practice wavering the tone evenly (using the vibrato technique of choice) at five or six pulses per second. Depending on the requirements of the music, a fine performer may use a slower or faster vibrato, but this frequency range represents the average for most performers.

Vibrato varies according to time period. For example, in the latter part of the nineteenth century and early part of the twentieth century, vibrato frequency and amplitude were much faster and wider than they are today. The vibrato used in the recordings of singers and instrumental performers of a century ago, such as cornet virtuoso and master pedagogue Herbert L. Clarke, is characterized as a "billy-goat" vibrato by today's standard. Classical players are expected to adapt their personal expression to match the style period and national origin of the piece they are performing—one would not play Mozart and Tchaikovsky the same way, for example—but they are not generally expected to revert to an older style of vibrato.

Vibrato also differs according to culture and nationality. In his excellent *The Trumpet* (1997), former principal trumpet of the London Symphony Howard Snell describes the vibrato created exclusively by the vertical movement of the chin as an outdated style in Britain associated with the brass bands of the 1930s to the 1970s, yet this is the predominant technique of the American style. He also states that the standard vibrato used in Britain today is a combination of chin movement and "the vibration of the airstream as it reaches the embouchure" (152). He does not explain this technique any further, but it seems to bear some resemblance to the breath impulse technique. Snell refers to the French vibrato of the early part of the twentieth century as "one of the most beautiful ever heard" (153), but expressive as it is, it is not the style preferred by most of today's classical trumpeters. Some believe that the recognizable distinctions between the national schools of expression and style will become a thing of the past as players gradually move to a single style of playing due to the influence of recordings by a handful of top performers.

Vibrato also differs according to musical genre. Jazz musicians are not constrained by the same conventions of conformity and style as classical musicians. Individual expression is the hallmark of the jazz musician, but vibrato is still determined to a degree by style and time period. There is a great difference between the 1950s West Coast cool style, a relatively vibratoless approach used by Miles Davis and Chet Baker, and the heavy vibrato of those who play in the early traditional style of the legendary Louis Armstrong.

Regarding vibrato and expression, Howard Snell advises that each player should develop his/her own way of expression. "The best ideas for all players are their own, born of their own musical feeling" (154).

5

Body Use

Refining Skill

One of the daily tasks that all serious performing artists face is the gradual winnowing away of parasitic tension. The process of overcoming habits of inefficient body use takes dedication and hard work. Although there are individuals whose form is correct from the start, for most of us, refining our skill is a lifelong process.

The achievement of poise, grace, and a relaxed flow in all of our actions is the mark of the expert, but so often we use our bodies in wrong, ineffective, and inefficient ways. The famed teacher at Northwestern University Vincent Cichowicz, said, "The struggle is not with the instrument, it is with ourselves."

The Goal of Efficient Performance

Aldous Huxley said, "In all activities of life, from trivial to important, the secret of efficiency lies in the ability to combine two seemingly incompatible states: a state of maximum activity and a state of maximum relaxation." But distinguishing between unnecessary tension and essential support requires careful experimentation. The most important question is how exactly do we go about achieving the goal of efficient performance?

Importance of Good Form

The great martial artist Bruce Lee maintained that the best form is the most efficient form, and this is true for the factory assembly line worker to the concert artist. When we strive to improve our form, we are striving for efficiency, even if we are unaware of it. Performing efficiently means using only the right amount of tension and only those muscles necessary. (See "Efficiency" in chapter 1.) Excessive body tension results in poor form, and poor form results in less than optimum performances. Physical efficiency is one of the most important aspects of skill to acquire, for without it every other parameter, from power to finesse, may be limited or even absent. Its importance cannot be overstated: virtually all of the techniques and ideas presented in this book, though they are ultimately at the service of expression, have greater efficiency as their goal.

Excessive Tension

Many players perform with some degree of excess or unnecessary tension. Author and Olympic athlete Dan Millman (1999, 73) said tension "leaks energy." Once the use of excessive tension becomes habitual, we are no longer aware of it. This "parasitic tension" is at the heart of most brass performance problems. The Valsalva maneuver, for example, one of the most common problems encountered by wind players, is activated by excess abdominal tension. (See "The Valsalva Maneuver" in chapter 3.) Using excessive amounts of tension in various parts of the body while performing reduces endurance, interferes with an open, clear sound, makes the upper register difficult or impossible, stiffens technique and fluency, and generally causes us to work much harder than necessary. The greatest athletes and performing artists are nearly always physically efficient, and we must emulate them in order to perform at the highest level of our potential.

Serious players eventually come to an awareness of the importance of efficient body use, typically later in their careers. As students, we are usually concerned with the more basic problems of physical performance, but as we refine our playing, we soon find the need to address more subtle aspects of form. We are like the athlete whose improvements are incrementally larger in the beginning, but as we reach the limits of our personal potential, a fraction of a second is hard fought. Attention to efficient form should not be put off until one has solved more pressing problems. If it is addressed early in a student's development, playing improvements will be swifter and greater and problems will be nipped in the bud.

Often a player will go through a period in which tension and poor playing habits build up through stress and fatigue, but this tension dissipates after a day or two of rest from the instrument. For this reason, many players take either a light day or a day off from playing once a week. Students who practice especially diligently can benefit from this kind of break, but they are typically the ones least inclined to take it.

EMG Biofeedback

According to James A. Howard (1991, 151), electromyographic (EMG) biofeedback training "may be an effective behavioral control technique for reducing excess muscle tension in musicians without compromising performance." Biofeedback therapy involves measuring bodily functions such as pulse rate and muscle tension through a device called an electromyograph. Changes within the body that are sometimes too subtle to detect can be identified with the help of the EMG; with this information, we can begin to change our reactions to particular stressors or stimuli. This technique has also been used to treat a wide range of disorders including anxiety and TMD, and it can be used to improve focus and concentration.

Learning to perform with less tension is the key to a higher level of performance. Ridding ourselves of automatic habits of excessive tension and force, however, is not easy. Each person has an individual pattern of body use whose path to improvement will be unique, but for virtually everyone the first place to look at is posture.

Posture and Tension

According to Daniel Kohut in his excellent *Musical Performance: Learning Theory and Pedagogy*, the primary source of excessive tension in physical performance is poor posture (1992, 67). Poor posture creates an imbalance in the body that requires extra tension to stabilize. In discussions of posture, the position of the head often receives the most attention. When the head is out of alignment, the balancing mechanism in the inner ear, called the vestibular mechanism, sends a message to the appropriate muscles to keep the body balanced, which results in added physical tension. If the head is perfectly balanced, then the player is capable of performing with greater efficiency. Kohut suggests that one of the best ways to teach good postural habits with young musicians is to have them stand during lessons and practice sessions. He believes that good playing position and general technique are better established and enhanced when a musician stands. Once poor posture has been learned and become automatic, however, it is difficult to change.

The Importance of Posture

When I stress the importance of good posture, someone always brings up the example of a fine player who sits or stands in what appears to be a very casual fashion and yet plays remarkably well. Many think of posture as rigid military-style "stomach in and shoulders back," but this is the antithesis of good performance posture. We are not seeking to find a particular pose and then freeze ourselves into position, but to find a way of using the body that is free of tension and the learned habits that cause us to hold the body in unnatural ways. For years I experimented with posture, and I found, through trial and error, a significantly improved ability to play.

Posture has always been one of the most important aspects in my physical performance technique. When I finally began solving some of the vexing problems I had fought for years, posture was a central issue. The position of my neck and head that I discovered through trial and error was especially important. I later learned that my discovery was consistent with the principles of body use in the teaching known as the Alexander Technique. When I brought my chest high (without bending backward) and my chin in, and most importantly, learned to relax my abdomen in that position, I discovered an ease of expression that included greater range and stamina. This single change made more of an immediate difference in my physical strength than anything else I had tried up to that point. When playing in the upper register, I felt I now had leverage, as if I had something to push against to give greater strength. Even today, after so many years of playing, the effect is quite concrete: with my learned upright posture, I have range and strength, but when I am even slightly slumped, it is diminished. Though others have noted this phenomenon, I have found that not everyone is so sensitive to posture. I believe that individuals who are more prone to poor posture, such as taller people, may be at more of a disadvantage, but this is speculation based solely upon my experience.

Our posture says a great deal about us. We unconsciously pick up cues from others through body language, and who we are and what we think is reflected in our posture. Do you stand tall and project confidence or slouch and project indecision and fear? Your posture is the direct manifestation of your inner feelings and mental state, and the reverse is also true: changing your body state can actually change your mental state. (See chapter 6.)

Finding Your Best Posture

Although it has taken me many years of patient trial and error to find my best performance posture, I recently discovered a shortcut.

1. Thinking of the lungs as a bellows, vigorously suck in and blow out a series of completely full breaths. (Stay by a chair in case of dizziness.) Try to get as much air in the lungs as you comfortably can by experimenting with putting the chest higher, dropping the shoulders, bringing the chin in, relaxing the abdominals, and stretching the spine to its longest point. Particularly notice the relaxed and stable feeling at the back of the neck and shoulders. Place the feet parallel, shoulder width, and unlock the knees.
2. When you are full of air, notice how you are holding yourself. Try to keep this same posture and head position when you exhale the air. If you are successful maintaining this posture, the shoulders and chest cavity will slightly fall as you exhale, but there will not be a slumping of overall posture or a change of head angle. Practice with this posture for a period of time and your results will determine whether it is worth pursuing.

This is a remarkably direct way to find your best playing posture, and it is easy to duplicate every time you play. Many players will feel instantly stronger and more balanced in this position, and some may realize an immediate improvement in sound, strength, accuracy, range, and general ease of playing. Repeating this sequence is an extremely important component of my warm-up, as it gets me actively blowing as well as in the proper posture for playing.

When you try this new position in your practice, be aware of the tendency during exhalation to slump forward or to let the chin come up and the head go back, especially when ascending into the upper register. Counteract this motion by remaining upright in your new posture. The angle that you normally hold your instrument may be changed due to the new head position. Note that one of the ways you will unconsciously return to your old posture is by assuming the old instrument angle.

Initially, you will need to hold yourself in the new position while fighting the tendency to return to your old posture. You will have to correct it each time you find you have unconsciously slipped back. The process of posture adjustment takes time, patience, and vigilance, but if you practice the new posture as your normal posture for daily life, you will learn it more quickly.

Your back may be tense after a long practice session from the contracted muscles holding you in a new position. This tension, like all excess tension, is ultimately undesirable, but it has an important purpose for a while. It functions the same way that a cast does on a broken bone: when the bone is healed, the cast comes off. Similarly, as soon as you begin assuming the new posture automatically, put your attention on consciously relaxing, but be sure you are not slipping back to your old habits. Learning to relax in the new posture is the most important step in the process. Without this, you are no better off than before. The very purpose of improving performance posture, after all, is to eliminate excessive tension, not add it.

If your back is stiff in the beginning stages, periodically get down on your hands and knees and practice the yoga exercise called the "cat back," which slowly alternates between an arched and concave back position to stretch tight muscles. Pilates, yoga, and other forms of physical exercise will help by strengthening and balancing the core muscles of the body to make it easier to relax and play with good posture. Try doing curls with free weights while maintaining this posture: inhale while curling the arms upward and then blow out through a small opening for four full curls or until the lungs are completely empty. Do not allow your posture to change as you reach the end of the breath. Two or three sets twice a week is very beneficial.

If you find that experimenting with posture interferes with your performing ability, reinforce it only during practice sessions until it is more automatic. One of the most efficient ways to establish new posture is to practice it while playing soft long tones. (See "The Twenty Minute G.")

The Shulman System

Owners of the Shulman System™ may find that discovering good performance posture is a significantly less labor-intensive process. Invented by jazz trumpeter Matt Shulman, the device claims to be a simple and effective way to improve playing efficiency by correcting posture. It is composed of a neck strap attached to a wooden device that rests upon the player's sternum and cradles the instrument. When properly adjusted, it reinforces efficient playing posture and body use, and prevents the player from unconsciously slipping back into poor playing habits. Because of the support the device offers, it is possible for many players to immediately play with a relaxed, correct posture and avoid the period of muscle tension and conflict that comes with replacing old postural habits.

In the short time that I have been experimenting with the device, I have been impressed with the ease and speed with which I was able to access the good posture that took me over forty years to learn. More information can be found at www.shulmansystem.com.

Lower Body Position

According to trumpet manufacturer and yoga instructor David Monette, the secret to a more efficient performance posture for many players lies in the lower body. It is common for players to lock their knees and position their feet with the toes angled outward, which adds unnecessary tension and places the body out of alignment. He suggests standing with the toes pointed forward and parallel about hip width apart with the knees unlocked or slightly bent. According to Monette, many of the world's greatest players display this stance, including Maynard Ferguson and Wynton Marsalis, and the higher they play into the upper register, the more they bend their knees. To prove this, Monette suggests taking a full breath while in your habitual stance and noting how high up in the chest the breath comes before it feels tight or full. Then, with the knees unlocked and the feet parallel, note how much more air you can take into the lungs beyond the previous stopping point. When sitting, as when standing, he recommends keeping the feet and thighs parallel and pointing forward. A little experimentation in your practice is the best way to find out if this idea has any value to you.

Seated Posture

With regard to the best posture when sitting, Arnold Jacobs suggested to "sit as you stand." If you are truly following this advice, you will be able to immediately stand from your seated position without having to uncross your ankles or shift your body forward.

According to Richard Norris (1993), musicians have a high incidence of lower and upper back pain largely because the human body was not designed to sit in modern chairs. Norris suggests that the flattening of the lumbar curve that occurs when sitting with the hips and knees bent at a 90-degree angle can be alleviated by the use of a wedge-shaped cushion or foam pad that elevates the buttocks at a 15- to 20-degree angle. He believes it is a better choice than the Scandinavian "kneeling" chair or chairs with a forward sloping seat because a cushion is more portable and less expensive.

Neck and Shoulder Pain

Pain in the neck and shoulders is a common complaint from musicians, and it is caused by two common postural bad habits: the slight forward jutting of the head and the raising of the shoulders. When I learned to release the tension in my neck and let my shoulders relax and find their proper place, the pain went away and my playing dramatically improved. Banishing this set of habits took a long time as I had to constantly remind myself, but it was a very important step in the improvement of my playing ability. This old pattern of tension comes back periodically during times of heavy stress, but it is welcome because it warns me that my posture has deteriorated and I am headed for trouble.

In *Treat Your Own Neck* (1998), physical therapist Robin McKenzie describes an exercise to help find the proper position of the neck relative to the spine. It involves retracting the head to the maximum degree possible so that the chin is pushed into the larynx. (I usually push the chin back with the side of my index finger.) McKenzie states that the ideal neck postural position is about 10 percent short of the extreme position. Through daily reinforcement of the head retraction exercise, we can learn to overcome the habitual jutting of the head that causes tension and pain. I usually do the exercise in the car or at the computer, and I can feel the lengthening of the muscles at the back of my neck that always tighten up when I am stressed. Armando Ghitalla often advised students to bring the chin in and "bury the head down."

Another beneficial posture exercise that I learned years ago from a physical therapist corrects slumping shoulders and head position. Lie on your stomach with both arms at shoulder level, elbows at right angles, and hands roughly even with the top of your head. Keep the head facing the floor but not touching it, with the chin in, and breathe normally. Keeping the arms parallel to the floor, raise them upward, and hold for a count of five. Rest and repeat ten times for a set. Doing two sets before bed every other night will strengthen the postural muscles that influence the correct position of the head, neck, and shoulders. Within a few days you may note it is easier to sit and stand more erect, and you may notice positive changes in your performance skill.

Experimenting with Posture

Finding and reinforcing the proper posture can take a long time. It must become automatic or it is of no use to you in performance. Constant attention during your warm-up and practice is required or you will revert to your old habits quickly. You will correct yourself a thousand times before you are able to assume the new posture without thinking about it. Since everyone is different, the only way to apply this principle is through trial and error. After a reasonable period, you will begin to notice that your sound will tell you if you are in doing things correctly.

The Alexander Technique

When F. M. Alexander began his search for answers to his problems, he found no relief in the limited medical and physiological knowledge of the late 1800s. A successful Shakespearean actor who was increasingly plagued with a loss of his voice during his performances, he began to study himself closely using mirrors and discovered a recurring habit of backward tilting of the head and downward pulling into the neck when he spoke. Alexander experimented with various ways of using his head and neck and soon found improvement in the function of his voice, eventually solving his problem. He noted that his tendency to pull his head backward and down adversely affected the rest of his body, and that he initiated this pattern of movement continually in everything he did. He believed that it had a deleterious effect on the health of the body and saw that people who employed this action did not notice it or associate it with the physical ills that plagued them. The movement was very subtle, and he might not have discovered it if its effect hadn't had such a dramatic impact on his career.

Alexander began work to reverse this habit by inhibiting his first response, to pull his head down and in, and learned to let his spine lengthen and his back widen. This use of the neck and head, which he called the "primary control," affected his entire body in positive ways.

How could a small, almost imperceptible contraction of the neck muscles have so much influence that it would prohibit a performing artist from doing his work?

The Primary Control

According to Sarah Barker, "The action that most often precedes wasteful or harmful responses is a contraction which pulls the head slightly backward and down. The effect of this is a compression of the spine, which, repeated hundreds of times a day over a span of many years, interferes with the smooth operation of the muscular and nervous systems and all the vital organs" (1981, 15). The answer to this problem of body use is simply to reverse the pattern: "As you begin any movement, or act, move your whole head upward and away from your whole body, and let your whole body lengthen by following that upward direction" (24). Alexander recognized this motion as the primary factor in organizing human movement and so termed it the "primary control." This contraction of the head and neck adversely affects the performance technique of millions of performers and is one of the principal causes of poor form.

Becoming aware of this destructive motion during your daily life is the first step in exorcising it. Be aware as you rise from a chair or walk up stairs, for example, to lead with your head rather than letting it fall back into your shoulders. While you play your instrument, drive your car, or brush your teeth, monitor your head position. Alexander practitioners suggest that you think about releasing your head, allowing it to move upward and away from your body and allowing your body to lengthen and widen as it follows the head. This is a very simple idea that will positively affect your body use in every way. Making the effort to get into the habit of being aware to lead with the head in all of your daily movements, from the moment you rise from bed until you lie down again, could be the very thing that moves you to a new level of performance ability. Unfortunately, our learned body habits make it difficult to change.

Faulty Sensory Input

Most of us carry far more muscle tension in our bodies than we need, and the Alexander Technique gives us a way to lessen areas of excessive tension. The Alexander student learns to cultivate a more natural alignment of the head, neck, and spine that produces better balance, strength, and coordination. These new skills allow one to move and carry out any activity, however simple or complex, with greater ease and less effort.

The difficulty in learning a new way to move and use our bodies is that our kinesthetic sense is faulty. We naturally use our bodies in the way that feels most natural, but this feeling is based in habitual, learned behaviors that are often a distortion of efficient and proper body use. We have all seen individuals who hold their bodies in what appear to be uncomfortable positions, but to that individual the habitual posture may feel right and even comfortable. Adopting another posture is a shot in the dark since we have nothing to base the correct posture upon other than our own habits.

Alexander believed that it is possible to make an unreliable kinesthetic sense reliable again, but it is difficult to do this when all we have to rely upon is the sensory information from our own bodies, which is based entirely on habitual use. The correct or right feeling of an action is not the proper gauge of body use. "When we stop doing the wrong thing," goes an Alexander Technique saying, "the right thing does itself."

Working with an Alexander Teacher

I have witnessed the extraordinary change in a musician's performance after working with an Alexander teacher. One of the most vivid experiences occurred at the International Trumpet Guild Conference in Akron, Ohio, in 1993. In her presentation, Barbara Conable, a well-known Alexander teacher and author, worked with a volunteer from the audience. The young man played an excerpt from the Haydn Concerto and then submitted to the very gentle hands-on manipulation that is characteristic of Alexander practitioners. After a few moments of adjusting his posture with Conable's help, the young man raised his instrument to his lips and played the same musical excerpt. The entire audience was stunned to hear the dramatic improvement in his sound and apparent ease of performance.

Vincent Cichowicz related a story about a young woman whose upper register on the trumpet was limited despite all of her efforts to improve it. Cichowicz had the opportunity to observe her session with an Alexander teacher, who determined that the young woman was contracting muscles in her neck and shoulder when she ascended in range, an action that had not been noticed by her teachers or even by the player herself. After some work with the Alexander Technique, her upper register improved rapidly, as did her sound and ease of response.

Application of the Technique

I have had the opportunity to study the Alexander Technique with a number of teachers over the years. The technique is not a way of holding oneself, nor is it a posture that is learned. It is a dynamic process of discovery in the moment that involves inhibition of the old response and the choice to move a different way. In order to produce results, according to those who work in this field, twenty to thirty lessons with an accredited Alexander teacher is a good estimate. I have found great benefits from my study of the technique, and I believe that anyone seriously seeking ways to improve performing skill would find this to be a very sound investment. (For more information, check the Alexander Technique Web sites on the Internet or see Barker 1981, Barlow 1990, Conable 1995, and Gelb 1987.)

Feldenkrais

Another effective method of identifying and correcting poor body use habits is the Feldenkrais Method. It was developed by Moshe Feldenkrais, a brilliant scientist with interests in fields as diverse as mechanical engineering, psychology, and martial arts. Feldenkrais can identify and retrain learned patterns of movement that are inefficient and contribute to pain and ill health. This is accomplished either through thirty- to sixty-minute sessions where groups are guided through a script that is organized around a particular function, or with a teacher who helps guide the body through gentle hands-on kinesthetic communication. Feldenkrais is a learning process, not massage or a therapeutic technique. To find out more about the Feldenkrais Method and locate a practitioner, go to http://www.feldenkrais.com.

The Twenty-Minute G

One of the most effective exercises to reinforce good posture and eliminate excessive tension is Cat Anderson's "twenty-minute G." Anderson, the famous lead trumpet of Duke Ellington's band, claimed that this exercise was his secret to playing high notes, but it is far more than that. Used consistently over time, it can overcome problems ranging from excessive mouthpiece pressure to poor response and lack of endurance. It also greatly enhances breath capacity and control of dynamic range and helps clarify the tone. In *The Cat Anderson Trumpet Method* (1973), Anderson instructed the reader to play a second-line G "like a whisper" for twenty minutes, but it is not a long setting exercise like those found in Carmine Caruso's teaching; the player can take the mouthpiece off the embouchure between tones.

Long tones have always been considered a basic and fundamental exercise for every brass player, but it seems that fewer students have the patience to do them today. It takes great personal discipline to do the twenty-minute G regularly. Though I could see the wonderful things it did for my own playing, there were times when I found it difficult to make myself do it. To make the task easier, many of the players I knew read the paper, did crossword puzzles, or watched TV when they did it. I found added benefit when I held each note to the end of my breath, which improved my breath control. Using a watch, I tried to improve my time and was eventually able to hold the G longer than two minutes consistently, although I could barely get past thirty seconds when I started. In performance, this allowed me to feel very comfortable and strong beyond the place where I normally took a breath.

While playing the G as softly as possible, it is relatively easy to pinpoint and eliminate unnecessary tension. Through the constant repetition of a more relaxed and efficient way of playing combined with good posture, we will eventually overcome excessive tension in our performance. The rewards of this effort can be quite dramatic for some players, particularly those who have been struggling for years with chronic problems rooted in excess tension. Occasionally, however, a player's problems are the result of too little physical effort.

Meeting the Effort Level of the Task

A few years ago I had a talented student with such poor range and endurance that he was unable to play through much of the standard literature on the trumpet. He was tall and willowy, and though he played occasional intramural sports, he was not given to regular physical exercise. On a whim, he accepted the invitation from one of our musicologists, an award-winning body builder, to work out regularly. Within three weeks, he demonstrated an astounding improvement in his physical performance ability by playing through two concertos during his lesson, including one on piccolo trumpet. This feat was impossible only weeks before, yet he had not made any change in his lifestyle or practice habits except that he was now working out every other day with an experienced weight lifter.

His improvement was something of a miracle to me. I had tried everything I knew to help him, but upon reflection it was clear that he simply had not been meeting the level of effort necessary to play the trumpet. Ironically, he was too relaxed and didn't realize that he needed to blow with more vigor and adopt a more energized state. Many performers are unaware they have this problem. When he began weight lifting, his personal energy level and strength were increased, and happily, he also remained relaxed and loose and did not introduce excess tension into his playing technique.

Occasionally I encounter players who put no more energy into performing on the trumpet than they might expend in a casual stroll across the park. Telling them to increase their energy level will often just introduce excess tension since they don't know how to channel the energy properly. A more effective way is to have them blow vigorously through the instrument or use an activation exercise to increase their arousal state. (See "Activation" in chapter 6.) Beginning a program of regular physical exercise would most certainly be a good idea. (See the "Value of Exercise.")

The Hands and Fingers

Jimmy Burke, the great cornet soloist, played with one hand because he was unable to use one of his arms. Over the years, I have known a few players who, for a variety of reasons, have found it necessary to use the left hand to manipulate the valves. It is clear that one does not need to hold or even work the valves of the trumpet in the conventional manner if it is physically not possible to do so. Some of the major manufacturers are willing, for a reasonable fee, to make a reverse trumpet or cornet with the valves on the opposite side of the leadpipe. There are also many talented repairpersons who can devise triggers and supports for students with disabilities. A former disabled student of mine used the Shulman System, described earlier in this chapter, to help support the instrument. The custom alteration of an instrument can sometimes mean the difference between enjoying musical performance and quitting music altogether.

The Right Hand

Most beginning trumpet and cornet players are taught to curl the fingers as if holding a softball and place the fingertips upon the valve buttons, but some players fall into the habit of pushing the little finger of their right hand all the way into the finger hook (or ring) and draping their fingers over the valves so that the knuckles push the valves down. This poor habit prohibits optimum fingering speed and precision. In order to change it, reinforcement of proper hand position using finger drills such as the Clarke *Technical Studies* (1912) is recommended until the new hand position becomes automatic.

The finger hook is often used incorrectly to assist in the forceful application of the mouthpiece to the embouchure. (For this reason, players facetiously call it the "octave key".) Some teachers encourage that the little finger be placed on top of the finger hook rather than in it at all times. The finger hook's primary function is to help the player hold the instrument with the right hand alone, such as when inserting a mute, but there is no real need to use it when performing. In extreme cases, I have taped a thumbtack inside the finger hook to stop students from using it to force the mouthpiece on the embouchure. This technique teaches the student to stop using the finger hook very quickly, but s/he may start using more left arm pressure to compensate. (See "Excessive Pressure" in chapter 4.)

The Left Hand

Some players grip the horn with the left hand forcefully, particularly when they are playing loud and high, but chronic use of the "death grip" on the instrument is a sure sign of excessive tension.

There is more than one proper left-hand position, and the best choice is a matter of personal preference. One of the most important considerations is the ease with which the hand position allows the fluent use of the first and third tuning slides. Most players use a "traditional grip" with all of the fingers of the left hand resting on the third valve slide and the thumb in the first trigger saddle or ring, or alternatively with the little finger (or more rarely two fingers) below the third slide. Some players use a "pistol" grip, popularized by the great Maynard Ferguson, with the thumb and forefinger circling the valve column and the rest of the fingers of the left hand below the third slide, as if holding a gun. This is usually favored by players who specialize in upper register playing and is rarely used by players who are not lead specialists.

Most players are taught the traditional grip and never think about it again, but occasionally a player can gain some advantage from experimentation with the left hand. The horn's angle is changed by the grip: the horn points downward at a steeper angle when all of the fingers are on top of the third slide than when they are below the slide. For this reason, some players might find that a new grip improves their performance because it changes the amount of pressure that comes to bear on the top or bottom lip.

The Arms

The arms should be relaxed and should hang naturally from the shoulders with the elbows bent to allow the hands easy access to the trumpet valves.

Some players raise their elbows high, even parallel to the ground with the hands severely bent backward at the wrist, but this arm position wastes energy and restricts the movement of the fingers.

Since the arms are the primary means to employ excessive force against the embouchure, relaxing the arms may help reduce pressure, but the only permanent solution is to establish a new habitual way of playing. (See "Excessive Pressure" in chapter 4.)

General Health

Those who do not take care of their bodies will ultimately find their performance adversely affected through low energy levels, illness, poor concentration, and other problems. The body cannot remain in a state of peak energy and good health forever. It must be cared for and maintained like the precious and delicate machine that it is. A balanced diet, plenty of water, rest, and regular exercise are important components of the healthy lifestyle that every serious performer must adopt and maintain. Regular maintenance, like the maintenance of a house, is the best we can do to remain active as players well into our later years.

The Value of Exercise

Playing the trumpet requires great strength and energy. The trumpet is one of the most labor-intensive musical instruments, especially when a performer is required to play high, loud, and long. Regular daily practice on the trumpet is required in order to perform at a minimum level of proficiency, but in addition to practice, a regular program of exercise is highly recommended for any performer with serious aspirations. There are dozens of excellent ways to maintain the health of the cardiovascular system, increase vital capacity, and maintain muscle tone.

After playing a concert, trumpet great Marvin Stamm retired to the home of his host, where the three of us talked until the early hours of the morning. He asked his host to wake him at 6 a.m. so that he might take his customary morning run, but we were sure he would sleep in that morning instead. To our surprise, he got up and did his daily workout. A successful professional player like Stamm knows the value of regular exercise. In the highly competitive environment of New York City, being in shape and ready for anything could mean the difference between working and not working. Self-discipline such as this is a characteristic of elite performers in every field.

Finding the Best Exercise for You

Finding the best kind of exercise for your body type, energy level, and temperament may take some experimentation. Bicycling, rowing, or swimming are excellent choices for the person who desires a low-impact type of physical activity, while others may enjoy more competitive activities such as tennis, racquetball, or martial arts. Jogging, walking, and jumping rope can be done with little or no equipment, and bicycling, cross-country skiing, and rowing can be done on machines and outdoors. Strength training with weights and exercise machines builds muscle mass and burns calories, and aerobic exercise is excellent for the heart and respiration. (The legendary principal trumpet of the Chicago Symphony, Adolf Herseth, recommended the Royal Canadian Air Force Exercise Plan.) Whatever the choice of exercise, it needs to be done regularly, such as two to three times a week, in order to be effective. A little exercise on a regular schedule has been shown to be much more beneficial than a lot of exercise on an irregular basis. The best way to ensure that it happens is to choose something you enjoy doing. If you don't enjoy doing it, you will eventually find reasons to stop.

Studies have shown that only 20 percent of men and 11 percent of women exercise enough for health benefits, and a lack of physical activity combined with a poor diet is a leading cause of death in the United States. The benefits of regular exercise include a longer lifespan and increased vigor and zest for life. Exercise has been proven to combat depression, anxiety, and stress. It reduces the risk of heart disease, stroke, high blood pressure, glaucoma, diabetes, and some forms of cancer, and it increases self-esteem and enhances self-concept. It will also enable you to play your instrument with greater ease and efficiency by improving posture and breath capacity and by reducing tension. It is truly amazing that all of these benefits cost only thirty minutes a day, three days a week. Why not start now?

Some Principles of Exercise

According to Mikesky (1997), in order to develop strength, we need to overload or stress our muscles beyond their normal load, and this should be done on a regular schedule with intervals of rest to allow the body to recover and rebuild. We should set the intensity or resistance level at about 80 to 90 percent of our maximal strength to produce the quickest results. Muscles adapt to their workload, so in order to get progressively stronger, the intensity, frequency, and duration of the workouts must increase over time. Maintaining strength is simply a matter of keeping a set program of exercise at the same level as long as the resistance or intensity is high enough to keep the strength the same. Some research indicates that after one has achieved the desired level of strength, only a single session per week is required for maintenance. This workout should be harder but shorter than normal with longer rest periods (Darden 1995, 60).

Arthur Jones, the inventor of the Nautilus exercise machine, said, "The human body is exercised best not by the volume of the work but by the energy put momentarily into that work" (Darden, 39). Jones was suggesting that our time could be spent most productively and efficiently by training harder for a shorter time period. This principle can be implemented by going through movements very slowly, coaxing as much energy out of the muscles as possible in the moment.

The loss of strength that normally occurs between ages thirty and eighty can be significantly slowed with regular exercise. The proof is overwhelming that lifelong exercise is one of the best habits one can develop for a full, productive, and happy life.

Progressive Overload

Many performers believe in the maxim "no pain, no gain," but there is a better way. In *How to Succeed in Sport and Life* (1999), Olympic champion Dan Millman states that with demands placed upon it, the body accommodates by getting stronger through the principle of progressive overload, but athletes often push themselves so hard that they are constantly fatigued and in pain. He says it is better to stay within one's comfort zone and allow overload to occur in small increments. "By staying within (but near the top of) their comfort zones, masters take a little longer to improve, but their improvements last longer" (11).

Yoga

Originating in India thousands of years ago, yoga is one of the most beneficial forms of exercise known. It requires no special equipment and can be practiced anywhere by persons of any age. Yoga consists of various postures that stretch, tone, and exercise the entire body in way that is gradual and low impact. The postures have a beneficial effect on the nerves, glands, and internal organs. Yoga also boosts physical vitality and energy, as well as banishing stress and tension. The regular practice of yoga teaches one to relax and to still the mind, both of which are critical for efficient, high-level performance. Yoga is a perfect form of regular exercise for many performing artists.

Tai Chi Chuan

Like yoga, tai chi chuan, known commonly as tai chi, is an ancient form of exercise that has great potential benefit for the body and mind. Once a secret and exclusive teaching in China, tai chi became widely known in the twentieth century. Unlike the primarily stationary poses of yoga, tai chi involves a series of movements and positions that flow in a connected fashion similar to martial arts. Often described as a form of "moving meditation," tai chi is known to improve the health of the general body and nervous system. Like yoga, it produces a calm and relaxed mental state and improves one's concentration, balance, flexibility, and coordination. Both yoga and tai chi are best learned from a teacher, but books and instructional videos can be found at bookstores and libraries.

The Pilates Method

Joseph Pilates (1880–1967) developed a method of mind and body conditioning that combines the mental centering and stretching benefits of yoga with the strength development of a weight resistance routine. Many of the exercises of the Pilates Method can be done on a mat without equipment, but there are more advanced exercises involving special apparatuses that Pilates invented. Pilates stated that the primary focus of the method was on the principles of concentration, control, centering, flow, precision, and breathing, resulting in a heightened sense of well-being and unity of mind, body, and spirit. Pilates movements are designed to correct muscle imbalances and improve the strength and flexibility of the body's core muscles, especially in the back and abdomen. The benefits of these relatively simple exercises include increased strength and flexibility, improved breath control, heightened energy and stamina, weight loss and body definition, improved posture, better focus and concentration, and increased core strength. Combining Eastern and Western principles of exercise and personal development, this popular and respected system is an excellent choice for a performing artist. There are dozens of books about Pilates available at bookstores and libraries, and classes can usually be found at health clubs, spas, colleges or universities, and YMCAs.

Diet

A sensible, balanced diet is often difficult to maintain, but good nutrition fuels the body. According to Anthony Robbins, most people don't understand the difference between good health and fitness and regularly confuse the two (Robbins 1991, 442). Fitness refers to one's capacity to be involved in physical activities, but health refers to the balance and optimal working of the body's circulatory, digestive, respiratory, and other systems. One can easily be in peak fitness but unhealthy.

Diet is one of the primary components of a healthy lifestyle. Eating as much water-rich food as possible each day, such as fruits and vegetables, is a simple guideline that has been shown to increase health and vitality. This is only true, however, if one is also using moderation in the consumption of refined sugar, alcohol, fried foods, and red meat.

Water

One of the most important components of a healthy diet is water. Water replenishes the body's fluids, promotes effective digestion, and washes toxins and impurities out of the system. When we have not had enough water, these toxins remain in our body. In addition, dehydration can produce a state of muscle weakness, dizziness, and irritability. Elite athletes know that high-level performance is not possible when the body is even slightly dehydrated. Gail Williams, former member of the Chicago Symphony Orchestra horn section, learned early of the importance of water in her diet and established the habit of drinking a glass of water every morning to start her day.

Drinking coffee, soft drinks, or alcoholic beverages will not produce the same beneficial effects as pure water.

Rest and Sleep

Sleep is a basic body function that can have a profound effect on one's performance. Sleep allows the repair of the body and restoration of energy and vitality. Without it, good health is impossible. Although mild sleep deprivation was shown in one study to have little effect on physical performance, it had a negative effect on cognitive ability, increasing the likelihood of concentration errors, poor decisions, and a general inability to think clearly (Kirschenbaum 1997, 84–85).

Young people are often unaware of the effects that sleep deprivation has on their performance ability. When a significant dip occurs in a student's playing, a lack of sleep is often part of the problem. Fine performers know the value of adequate rest before important performances because they have learned the hard way: one is sharp and able to perform at his/her highest level only when the body is energized through adequate rest and sleep.

Teeth and Gums

The gums and teeth require our care and attention now or they will demand it later. Daily brushing, flossing, and regular prophylactic care from a dentist are a must for a brass player's very survival. In his book *Jazz and Death*, Frederick Spencer lists a large number of musicians, mostly brass players, whose careers and even lives were cut short because of problems with their teeth. Proper gum and dental care will not guarantee freedom from problems, but a failure to do all we can is practically an invitation to trouble.

Musician's Injuries

According to Alice G. Brandfonbrener of the Northwestern University Medical School, editor of the journal *Medical Problems of Performing Artists*, as many as 76 percent of musicians have suffered occupational injuries or illnesses that adversely affected their playing (Brody 1989). In one recent study of over 2,200 symphony and opera musicians, 67.5 percent reported musculoskeletal problems, with the largest number of these complaints located in the neck and/or back, followed by the arms, shoulders, hands, and wrists. In addition, a substantial number of performers report stress-related problems, including stage fright, depression, sleep disturbances, and acute anxiety.

Interest from the medical establishment concerning the problems of performing artists has been increasing since the 1960s, and performers today are finding competent and knowledgeable assistance for their occupational injuries and illnesses from a growing number of health professionals who specialize in the treatment of performing artists. Many musicians' journals now carry columns and articles on medical topics. It should be noted that in 1980, the *International Trumpet Guild Journal*, with Leon Whitsell as medical advisor, became the first musical instrument periodical to carry a regular column discussing medical research of special interest to its readers.

Common Trumpet Player's Injuries

While other instrumentalists' most commonly reported physical injuries are to the back, neck, shoulders, arms, and hands, trumpeters primarily suffer from problems of the embouchure, face, oral cavity, jaw, and teeth. The lips are especially vulnerable to a host of potential problems, such as physical trauma, nerve damage, infection, and metal-induced allergy. Disorders such as TMD, Bell's palsy, incompetent palate, and neck hernia are also fairly common to brass players, but their understanding, prevention, and cure are far from well-known to the average player.

Playing the trumpet produces the highest reported intrathoracic pressure of any instrument, but beyond the possibility of fainting due to rapid and extreme changes in blood pressure (syncope), problems related to the respiratory system from playing are considered nominal (Faulkner and Sharpey-Schafer 1959). There is no research to date showing that the high intrathoracic pressure of high brass playing directly causes hernias, headaches, or hemorrhoids, but a recent study of the increases in intraocular (eye) pressure caused by trumpet performance concluded that there is a small but significant increased risk of visual field loss and glaucoma related to the cumulative amount of trumpet performance over time (Schuman et al. 2000).

Embouchure Injuries

When serious injury to the embouchure occurs, it can keep a player from working for an indefinite period or even permanently end a career. Serious injuries can be largely avoided through commonsense precautions and by being aware of the body's signals. In general, when you have been reduced by fatigue to playing with brute force to produce a tone, it is long past the time to stop and take a rest. Flexibility and response will be greatly enhanced at the next session if you do a slow, soft warm-down, including pedal tones and chromatic scales, before putting the instrument away. If pain lasts for more than twenty-four hours or if performance ability has been significantly affected and/or there are no signs of recovery, a medical professional should be consulted. It is vital that players learn that whenever there is pain in the embouchure, it is time to stop playing.

Nerve Compression

Brass players are particularly susceptible to nerve compression injuries when the mouthpiece is excessively forced on the embouchure. (See

"Compression by Force" in chapter 3.) Chronic compression can reduce or stop the nerve's ability to transmit electrical impulses. The symptoms of this type of injury are tingling, pinching, sharp pain, slight numbness, and eventually embouchure dysfunction due to a complete loss of sensation. Minor injuries will usually heal with the elimination of force to the nerve, but if the player does not heed the signals from the body in time, permanent nerve injury could occur, resulting in a lack of sensation at the compression point. Players who feel the symptoms described earlier should discontinue playing immediately and rest, and those with chronic pain and numbness should seek a specialist. Often a change in the angle of the mouthpiece to the embouchure is necessary to completely eliminate the problem.

Muscle Tears

Tearing of the *obicularis oris*, known as Satchmo's Syndrome, can occur when the muscle tissue is subjected to unusually severe stress or trauma. Players who find they can no longer pucker firmly, who have an air leak in the embouchure when one hadn't existed before, who find it painful to play, or who experience a relatively sudden lack of range and endurance may be victims of this condition. Although it has been successfully repaired a number of times through surgery, there is no guarantee that performing ability can be restored. (For more information, see the December 1982 and May 1996 *International Trumpet Guild Journal* describing Dr. Jaime Planas's efforts to help brass players afflicted with Satchmo's Syndrome.) The only real way to avoid this serious injury is to eschew the use of damaging force at all costs.

TMD and TMJ

TMD, or temporomandibular disorder, is the name for a group of disorders that affect the temporomandibular joint (TMJ or jaw joint) and all of the muscles that open and close the jaw. (It is known as CMD, or craniomandibular disorder, in Europe.) TMD can be caused by a number of factors, including an injury, disease, malocclusion of the teeth, and jaw clenching and teeth grinding caused by stress. There are three categories of TMD: myofascial pain, which is chronic pain and discomfort in the muscles of the jaw and possibly the neck and shoulder; internal derangement of the TMJ, or a dislocation of the jaw and other problems in the jaw joint; and degenerative joint disease such as osteoporosis or rheumatoid arthritis.

TMD is most prevalent among brass, violin, and viola players, and more common among women than men. The signs of TMD include jaw pain when chewing which can radiate to the face, neck, and shoulders; locking or limited motion of the jaw; painful clicking, popping, or grinding when opening the jaw; head- and earaches; dizziness; difficulty hearing; and a change in the bite or fit of the teeth. Clicking or popping of the jaw is very common and not necessarily a sign of trouble, but if this is accompanied by chronic pain, a specialist should be consulted.

Often the symptoms of TMD are temporary, and a conservative and reversible treatment is recommended, including relaxation and stress-reduction techniques, moist heat packs, soft foods, and avoiding extreme movements of the jaw. More extended treatment can include gentle physical therapy, muscle relaxants, and anti-inflammatory drugs. Surgery should not be considered until all less invasive treatments have been explored, and seeking a second opinion is strongly advised.

Dry Mouth

Some players have great difficulty performing due to dry mouth, or the inability to produce saliva. This is almost always a temporary reaction to stress. (It is not the same as the serious condition called xerostomia, or chronic dry mouth, whose sufferers can experience cracked lips, mouth sores, a burning sensation in the throat, and other symptoms.) One solution for nervous dry mouth suggested by Maurice André is to lick fingertips that have been dipped in lemon juice, but most players may find it simpler to have water available. Hypnosis and relaxation techniques may help alleviate this condition.

Hearing Loss

Significant hearing loss can spell the end of a professional musician's career, but most musicians are completely unaware that they may be putting their hearing in jeopardy every day. While there is no question that rock musicians and others who play amplified electronic instruments have a higher incidence of noise-induced hearing loss than the general public, studies show this is also true for professional classical musicians. Sitting next to high-decibel-producing instruments in an orchestral setting would seem to be the primary cause, but one should not discount the damage that can be done to the delicate inner ear by practicing a piccolo trumpet into a music stand in a small room.

Hearing loss can be caused by such factors as high decibel sound, physical injury, aging, disease, heredity, and use of ototoxic drugs, including some antibiotics and diuretics. Tinnitus, or ringing in the ears, follows exposure to loud noise and may be a sign of hearing damage. It is usually temporary, but it could become permanent over time if care is not taken to protect the ears. Although *conductive* hearing loss (referring to problems with the outer or middle ear such as a damaged ear drum) is often treatable, *sensory* hearing loss is generally considered permanent: once the delicate hair cells within the cochlea are damaged, they cannot be repaired.

Roger Stoner, former professor of trumpet at the University of Kansas, was unable to continue playing and teaching after a thirty-two-year career due to intolerable pain and ringing in his ears (Stoner 2001). Stoner stated that although he may have been genetically predisposed to hearing loss, the severe damage to his inner ear was the direct result of "performing, teaching and practicing the trumpet in a confined space over many years" (71). Stoner concludes that his hearing problems probably could have been prevented through the use of "a more suitable teaching and practicing environment," and he believes that "most, and perhaps all teachers of music are at risk for hearing impairment."

Several years ago I had my hearing tested and found that I had a "moderate, high frequency sensorineural hearing loss" in my right ear. Since my trumpet students always sit on my right, it seemed likely that this loss was the result of my occupation. I found that I could not teach with the protective ear plugs recommended by the clinic, but I have begun to take better care of my hearing by asking students to point their instrument away from me and avoiding playing directly into the music stand. It has always been my habit to practice late at night while my family slept, so I have become used to playing with a practice mute, which has no doubt helped me avoid more potential hearing loss. Although I dislike wearing ear plugs, I always carry them with me in the event that I find myself at a job with a cymbal next to my ear. These simple cautions could save me from wearing an amplification device within a few short years.

Incompetent Soft Palate

The soft palate is the fleshy part of the inside of the mouth that arches downward from the hard palate (roof of the mouth) into the throat. In this area there is a flap that acts as a trap door, opening and closing to allow air to flow into the nasal passages or to stop that flow as needed for speech. It is possible for that flap to leak, from birth, trauma, allergies, or surgery, including a tonsillectomy and removal of wisdom teeth. This is known as an *incompetent palate, stress velopharyngeal incompetence,* or *soft palate inadequacy*. Individuals with this problem find that as they ascend into the upper register, the air pressure within the oral cavity can give way, sometimes manifesting itself as a snort or explosion of air into the nasal passages. With the air leaking through the nasal passages, it is impossible to generate the inter-oral pressure needed to play loud and/or in the upper register.

A speech aid prosthesis (palatal lift) can cure the problem of an incompetent palate in a wind instrumentalist. Also called a speech bulb or prosthetic speech appliance, this device can perform the miracle of enabling performance to one who has been unable to play into the upper register. Looking something like a traditional wire-and-plastic dental appliance or retainer, the prosthesis fits against the roof of the mouth and a small bulb holds the palate closed. A former student discovered that a leaking soft palate was the cause of her lifelong struggle to play. She was immediately able to perform successfully after a prosthesis was made.

David G. Dibbell of the University of Wisconsin Medical Center has successfully treated several musicians with this problem through surgery. The procedure has been used for decades for children with cleft palates, and though Dr. Dibbell does not believe everyone can benefit from the surgery, he estimates that as many as 70 to 75 percent will find their careers saved through this alternative (Dibbell 1978, 25).

The incompetent soft palate may be more common that we think, but undiagnosed or misdiagnosed palate leaks are a large part of the problem. Players or teachers who suspect the palate is the cause of performance difficulties should contact a professional who can properly diagnose and treat the condition.

Bell's Palsy

The seventh cranial nerve (CN-VII) is known as "the nerve of facial expression" because it allows us to express emotions through our faces. It contains about ten thousand individual fibers that transmit nerve impulses from the brain to the muscles of the face, as well as to the tear and saliva glands, and to the stapes in the middle ear; and sensations of taste from the forward portion of the tongue. In its path between the brain and the face, the facial nerve passes through an inch-and-a-half-long canal in the temporal or ear bone. If this nerve is damaged, inflamed, or irritated through trauma, virus, infection, tumor, surgery, or extreme temperatures, it can result in spasms, twitching, weakness, loss of control, or paralysis of the face. One of the most common disorders of the facial nerve is Bell's palsy, caused by the swelling of the facial nerve within the temporal canal, which damages the nerve and results in facial paralysis. Treating the cause of the problem is the usual cure, but sometimes the cause is unknown. (A similar but much rarer condition is trigeminal neuralgia, an affliction of the trigeminal nerve that transmits sensation to the face. The symptoms include sharp and often excruciating pain at the mouth and jaw.)

I have been acquainted with three individuals who were afflicted with Bell's palsy, and in all three cases the condition vanished completely after a period of time without invasive medical treatment. Sometimes, however, the condition is permanent. Typically, one side of the face is paralyzed and without expression. The eye must be protected or even taped shut because blinking is diminished or disabled, and the tear ducts do not provide tears. It may take many months after the primary effects of the condition subside before full performance ability is restored, and it is possible that one will have to relearn how to play on the afflicted side of the face.

Bell's palsy is a serious condition that requires the attention of a doctor, and it is advisable to get a second opinion on any recommended treatment. There is no immediate cure; one must simply wait patiently for the facial nerve to heal.

Collapsed Lung

Pneumothorax, commonly known as collapsed lung, is a condition in which air gets in the pleural space between the lung and chest wall, preventing the lung from expanding and causing the lung to collapse on itself. The symptoms are a sudden sharp pain, difficult or rapid breathing, and coughing. It is possible the chest will look unsymmetrical. The cause of a spontaneous collapsed lung is often unknown, but smokers and people with asthma, pneumonia, and other respiratory system diseases are at a higher risk. Diagnosis and treatment include a chest X ray, a chest tube that sucks out the air that is surrounding the lung, and a pain killer. A small collapse may fix itself in time, but for a large collapse that is causing breathing problems, hospitalization will be required. It is interesting that a large number of the eight to nine thousand victims in the United States each year are tall, thin males between twenty and forty years of age.

Throat or Neck Hernia

A player whose neck bulges exaggeratedly while playing may have a neck hernia, or pharyngeal pouch. (The throat normally bulges to some degree during strenuous playing, but a neck hernia may resemble Dizzy Gillespie's herniated cheeks.) This condition is caused by the high inter-oral pressures generated by trumpet playing combined with a chronic poor head position, such as raising the chin, that leaves the throat vulnerable to injury. There are many fine performers with this condition, and it does not affect their performing ability. According to Dibbell (1978, 24–25), the neck hernia is considered harmless, does not cause pain, and is usually better left alone. Performing with the proper head and neck position is the way to avoid a neck hernia.

Dystonia

Dystonia is a neuromuscular condition that causes involuntary, abnormal contractions of the muscles. This disease often manifests itself when the individual is involved in specific tasks or using specific groups of muscles, such as using the hands to play the piano or forming an embouchure to play a brass or woodwind instrument. In the case of a brass player with embouchure dystonia, the muscles of the mouth, jaw, tongue, and face may not respond, resulting in air leaking from the corners of the embouchure, uncontrolled puckering, and involuntary closing of the mouth; there may also be tremors, twitching, and spasms. This condition is a disaster to performance skill, but the onset effects are sometimes so subtle that it is very difficult to detect.

At present there is no cure, but certain oral medications and Botox (botulinum toxin) injections are currently being used to alleviate the symptoms. Richard Lederman (1991, 197) noted that taking a rest from performing "has not been particularly useful" at alleviating the symptoms of dystonia and cited a horn player whose cramp instantly reoccurred after twelve years of abstinence from playing the instrument. Joseph F. Phelps, former professor of trumpet at Appalachian State University, was forced to retire from a thirty-year teaching career after he was afflicted with this illness at age forty-nine. According to Phelps (2002), dystonia is six times more common than Lou Gehrig's disease or muscular dystrophy, but fewer than 5 percent of the individuals who are afflicted receive a correct diagnosis. The Dystonia Medical Research Foundation can be found at www.dystonia-foundation.org.

Finding Help

If you are having difficulty playing because of a physical or psychological problem, a good first step is to research the possible cause and recommended routes for relief. There are several excellent books and sources about musician's injuries and injury prevention, but especially recommended are Nicola Culf's *Musicians' Injuries: A Guide to Their Understanding and Prevention* (1998), Janet Horvath's *Playing (less) Hurt: An Injury Prevention Guide for Musicians* (2002), Richard Norris's *The Musician's Survival Manual: A Guide to Preventing and Treating Injuries in Instrumentalists* (1993), and Robert T. Sataloff, Alice G. Brandfonbrener, and Richard J. Lederman, editors, *Textbook of Performing Arts Medicine* (1991).

Clinics that specialize in performing artists' injuries and illnesses have grown tremendously since the turn the century. A list may be found at http://yourtype.com/survive/clinics_for_performers.htm. Links to performance arts medicine sites may be found at www.ithaca.edu/faculty/nquarrie/related.html. To find the names of medical practitioners for performing artists, contact the Performing Artists Medical Association (PAMA) at artsmed@aol.com.

6

Performance Psychology

The Mental Aspects of Performance

Research from the partnership of sport and science has given the performing arts an understanding of how the mind functions in high-level performance and specific ways to train the mind to enhance performance ability.

Gaining control of the mental aspects of performance is an important contributing factor in the success or failure of any performer. Finding a teacher or coach who puts the same emphasis on mental skill as on physical skill is extremely rare. Players whose performance problems are rooted in the mental aspects of performance often learn to cope through hard and unpleasant lessons. This approach can contribute to a decline in a player's enjoyment and interest in performance and may lead to an avoidance of performing altogether.

Mental Control

Although a player may practice diligently for months to prepare for an important performance and eventually arrive at the absolute peak of his/her ability, it is possible for the performance to go very badly. Even individuals with highly developed physical skill are at the mercy of the mental aspects of performance. Without mental control, there can be wide fluctuations of ability and consistency within a single performance or from performance to performance. The ability to concentrate and focus in the moment, as well as to control one's thoughts, is a characteristic of all great performers. These traits can and must be learned in order to perform at the highest levels. A whole new world of proficiency is possible once we learn to control the mental aspects of performance.

Flow

While involved in performing at the top of their ability, elite athletes have reported certain kinds of inner sensations and experiences that are consistent with those of musicians and other performing artists. They include a total immersion in the activity, a feeling of effortless mastery and control, an extremely confident mindset with no thoughts of fear or failure, a sense of being physically energized combined with joy or deep peace, and a narrow focus of attention on the here and now. Others report almost metaphysical sensations, including a sense of time slowed or suspended and a feeling of being unified or an integral part of the world around them. These feelings and experiences are not present during every performance but characterize peak or optimal performances. Sports psychologists have learned that a performer has a greater probability of success if s/he can trigger and maintain this kind of state during performance, and that is exactly what mental training is for.

These characteristics of elite performers are representative of an optimal state of experience researcher Mihaly Csikszentmihalyi (1990) calls "flow." Flow can be described as the feeling during performance when the mind is completely focused in the moment and the body is working effortlessly and harmoniously with the environment. Performers who experience flow are completely in control of what they are doing. Flow is one of the most enjoyable states a human being can know, and seeking ways to the flow state is the reason that most of us engage in sports, music, dance, painting, chess, and other activities.

Flow is the ability to find happiness in the experiences of the moment. The inner harmony that comes from flow can be obtained from the simplest experiences. According to Csikszentmihalyi, flow requires a goal, a way to measure the progress to the goal, the maintenance of concentration on the goal, the commitment to make finer distinctions in the challenges of the goal, the development of skills to meet the challenges, and the desire to look for other challenges when the goal has been met. One of the keys to finding flow is the balance between one's skill level and the challenge of the particular task at hand. For example, if a task is too difficult or too easy relative to a performer's skill level, flow will be more difficult to achieve. An *autotelic* experience, or one that is intrinsically rewarding and done for its own sake, is the type of task that leads to flow experiences.

Work that is laborious or boring to one person can be pleasurable to another depending on one's orientation to the task, and that is the secret of flow. We can find complexity, challenge, and beauty in the simplest acts, whether driving to the store or working in the garden. Flow is possible at any moment. Some people who continuously live in a state of flow can't distinguish between work and play and would choose to continue to live the life they have chosen even if they were offered fame and riches. When we are aware of the joy of flow experiences, we tend to try to repeat them. The secret to the flow state is living fully in the here and now.

Performing in the Now

We all know the pleasurable feeling derived from doing something well, completely focused in the moment, without any background noise from the mind. It is often described as being in the groove, in the zone, having a flow experience or a peak performance. It is the reason many of us are performers, but we don't know how to produce this state at will. Control of our thoughts is the key.

According to spiritual teacher Eckhart Tolle (1999), instead of dwelling in the now, the only place where anything real can happen, the average person is constantly thinking about the past and future by reliving past experiences and imagining largely worrisome future outcomes. The mind constantly holds our attention with a never-ending stream of analysis, judgments, comparisons, labels, condemnation, and praise. Poor control over our own thoughts is a primary cause of performance problems because our attention is not directed where it should be: on what we are doing.

In *The Mastery of Music,* Barry Green (2003) quotes Armando Ghitalla, former principal trumpet of the Boston Symphony, as saying "it is important to approach playing with an uncluttered mind." Ghitalla goes on to say "It helps to have a mental exercise to shut out intruding thoughts that have little or nothing to do with music making" (207). Charles Schleuter, the current principal trumpet of the Boston Symphony Orchestra, states, "There is no anxiety in the present. Anxiety is either in the past, worrying about what was just played, or in the future, worrying about what you are about to play" (Green, 197). He also advises, "Don't judge or evaluate while you're performing" (197).

Try this test of your ability to control your thoughts: while playing a soft long tone, keep your attention focused closely on the sound of the note. Make yourself aware of your entire body as it is engaged in playing the note. Be as present in the moment as possible. Think of nothing, just observe. If you can remain in this state of focused attention for longer than a few seconds without your mind chiming in with a commentary on the situation, then you are above average. (This is a highly recommended way of practicing long tones.)

When you observe a great artist giving an inspiring performance, you are hearing someone who is performing in the now and able to remain there. Individuals who have achieved mastery in any field of endeavor have learned the ability to closely focus their attention on what they are doing. Eugen Herrigel (1971) speaks of Zen monks using the art of archery to achieve this state. Though it is possible for anyone to perform with this kind of disciplined attention, most players haven't learned the skill yet. It takes practice to learn to still the mind, and the prototypical exercise that human beings have used for centuries for this purpose is called by various names, including meditation, contemplation, and prayer. (See "Meditation.")

Before we discuss ways to control the mind, let us look at the biggest psychological barrier to performance: fear.

Performance Anxiety

The greatest psychological problem that the average performer faces is fear, or more accurately, the body's responses to fear. It is a rare performer who has not known "butterflies in the stomach," but for some the problem is much more exaggerated. Symptoms can include muscle rigidity, trembling, sweating, dry mouth, headache, upset stomach, nausea, dilated pupils, cold extremities, hair standing on end, racing heartbeat, extreme pallor or flushing of the face, a need to evacuate the bowels, poor concentration, deep sighing, yawning, and shallow, rapid breathing. Others may also have a strong emotional response, including anxiety, depression, hopelessness, sadness, frustration, anger, and dread. For some performers, the physical and emotional effects of so-called performance anxiety are so intense that they seem impossible to overcome. It is not uncommon for musicians to so dislike performing because of these feelings and the resultant poor performances that they will avoid performing or quit music altogether.

Fight or Flight

What we call performance anxiety is actually the body's automatic and involuntary response to an attack on our survival, whether real or imagined. The symptoms of performance anxiety are simply the body's preparation to fight or run away, so it is known as "fight or flight syndrome." Originally discovered by Harvard physiologist Walter Cannon, this response is genetically hard-wired into our brains and is designed to protect us from bodily harm.

An almond-shaped area in the center of the brain called the amygdala is the body's command center when a threat is perceived. Though we may consciously realize that we are in no real danger, fear can still cause changes in the body even when we don't want them to happen. Because the amygdala is connected to the entire body via a complex network of nerves, it can trigger a bodywide state of emergency in a split second. The amygdala orders the part of the brain stem called the hypothalamus to produce the hormone corticotropin releasing factor (CRF), which in turn tells the adrenal glands to release adrenaline, noradrenaline, norepinephrine, and cortisol. It also activates the pituitary gland to produce oxytocin and vasopressin. These powerful hormones cause the body to rapidly undergo a series of dramatic changes that include doubling to tripling the resting heart and respiration rate, dilation of the coronary arteries, shunting of the blood from the digestive tract and internal organs to the muscles and limbs, dilation of the bronchial tubes and the pupils of the eyes, the release of blood sugar into the blood stream, and the secretion of hydrochloric acid in the stomach.

Within seconds our awareness intensifies, our sight and hearing sharpen, our impulses quicken, our perception of pain diminishes, and we become prepared both physically and psychologically to fight or run. The capillaries under the surface of our skin are constricted so we can sustain a surface wound without major loss of blood, and all unnecessary bodily functions, including digestion and reproduction, are shut down. The stomach may also disgorge its contents, and bodily waste may be eliminated involuntarily. It doesn't matter that one is in no real physical danger while standing on the stage facing an audience; our bodies respond to real or imagined threats in the same way. Although this response could save your life, it is inappropriate and counterproductive in the context of a musical performance. We must teach our body another strategy that will help rather than hinder our efforts to function effectively as performers.

Fear Conditioning

When we encounter a situation that frightens us or causes us pain or discomfort, the brain, under direction from the amygdala, stores a strong memory of the experience as well as the circumstances under which it occurred. These memories can easily be triggered by cues associated with the event, quickly sending the body back to a state of alert. For example, if a performer has an embarrassing disaster on the concert stage, the thought of being on stage can trigger the body's fight or flight mechanisms. For some individuals, fear can be associated with seemingly ordinary occurrences, resulting in debilitating phobias, stress disorders, or constant low-grade anxiety. Prolonged exposure to stress-producing hormones has been shown to adversely affect the body, from high blood pressure, ulcers, and reduced memory capacity to impaired immune system, heart disease, and possibly even cancer. In other words, victims of constant fear and stress are much more susceptible to illness and even death.

Beta-Blockers

Beta-blockers are drugs that block the action of stress hormones at special sites (beta receptors) throughout the body. By blocking the action of adrenalin's affects to the muscles, for example, they can slow the heart, widen the arteries, and lower blood pressure. Beta-blockers are principally used to lower blood pressure, correct irregular heartbeats, and reduce heart problems. They are also used for migraines, glaucoma, hyperthyroidism, and for their unique ability to stop the effects of fight-or-flight symptoms on the body. Many professional musicians use these drugs in order to counteract performance nerves, and they are very effective for this purpose.

Beta-blockers do have some occasional side effects, including disorientation, dizziness, difficulty concentrating, hallucinations, lowered libido, and shortness of breath. They can be very dangerous if used improperly: asthmatics, diabetics, and individuals with heart diseases could become gravely ill or die when using beta-blockers. These are prescription drugs and should be used under a doctor's supervision.

There are many beta-blockers available, but the one used most often by performers is propranolol hydrochloride, which is distributed as Inderal. The musicians I know who use this drug take a much smaller dose than is prescribed for high blood pressure. If you wish to try this medication, it is important to find a physician who knows something about the specific application of Inderal for performance anxiety.

There are some who suggest that it is wrong to use drugs as a performance "crutch" or that it is somehow cheating to use beta-blockers to alleviate the negative effects of fear on performance skill. Deciding that beta-blockers are the best choice for overcoming debilitating performance anxiety is the business of no one but the performer and his/her doctor. However, one should be well informed of the dangers of these drugs. According to Irmtraud Tarr Krüger (1993), regular use of beta-blockers can make one more sensitive to adrenaline, causing an increase in anxiety symptoms; problems with dependency, including serious withdrawal symptoms, are also possible. In *Performance Power*, Krüger (1993, 102) offers her own safe and effective alternative to beta-blockers: two teaspoons of liquid lecithin, two teaspoons of sea-buckthorn juice (hippophaë rhamnoides, available in health food stores), and twenty-five drops of lemon oil.

Many believe that musical expression is dampened or altered when beta-blockers are used. Taking the edge off of a performance may seem an advantage at the outset, but as we shall see shortly, a low level of arousal can have a negative impact on performance. (For more information on beta-blockers, see Brantigan and Brantigan 2000.)

The Body/Mind Connection

In *Beyond Biofeedback* (1977), researchers Elmer and Alyce Green discuss the results of their study of the effects of mind control on the body. While carefully monitoring the bodily functions of yogis from India, they determined that it is indeed possible to consciously change not only breathing and heart rate, but brain wave patterns, blood pressure, and body temperature. They also found that it is possible to teach others to control their bodily processes because each of us has the same potential ability as the yogis. The Greens' study highlights the connection between the mind and body, showing that changes in our mental or emotional state result in changes in the body. The reverse of this principle is also true: changes in the body can elicit changes in our emotional states.

Overcoming Fear

Edmund Jacobson (1930, 1976), a well-known researcher and author of several books on the relationship of mind and body, stated that if the physical effects of an emotion are eliminated from the body, then the emotion itself will be eliminated. This suggests that one way to eliminate emotions not conducive to optimal performance is to learn to become relaxed and calm. Most people find it very difficult to relax on command, but it is possible with repeated practice to program the brain through the use of certain exercises to quickly attain the desired mental state.

Controlling the Breath

The optimal integration of mind and body necessary for peak performance can't occur without a relaxed body and focused mind, and controlling the breath is one of the simplest and most direct ways of achieving this state. Rapid, shallow breathing is a characteristic of fight-or-flight syndrome and a sure indicator that one is stressed and fearful. Although it is extremely difficult to control one's instinctive reactions, taking control of the breath is one thing that can help to quickly calm a player in the moment. When faced with a situation that causes fear or panic responses in the body, simply breathe deeply and slowly. Changing rapid, shallow breathing to deep, slow breathing will change your physiological state for the better. (Use diaphragmatic breathing rather than chest breathing as described in "The Lungs" in chapter 1.)

A sigh will also help to release tension. Take a deep breath, relax, and sigh through a small opening in the lips. Don't blow; just let it go. This is a simple idea with great to power to aid a performer in distress by bringing the body to a relaxed state. (See "The Sigh" in chapter 1 and "Triggers, Cues, and Anchors" later in this chapter.) However, there are more permanent and effective solutions to the problem of performance anxiety.

The Relaxation Response

In the mid-1970s, Herbert Benson (1979) proposed that the body has an innate and natural relaxation response that produces changes in the body that are the exact opposite of the fight-or-flight response. The body's ability to reach this state of extremely low arousal is controlled by the hypothalamus at the base of the brain, the same organ that activates fight-or-flight symptoms. Its purpose is believed to be restorative and a natural protection against overstressing the body. The relaxation response produces decreases in muscle tension, breathing and heart rate, blood pressure, and body metabolism, and an increase in alpha waves in the brain. All of these are the polar opposite of the changes in the body produced by fight-or-flight syndrome.

Benson's original studies were with subjects who practiced Transcendental Meditation. This was the route to the relaxation response that he originally advocated, but he later discovered that any form of meditation or relaxation technique was effective in eliciting this deep state of relaxation.

Meditation

For centuries, mystics, yogis, monks, and martial artists have sought to tame the chaotic flow of thoughts in the mind to reach a high degree of mental clarity and awareness. Meditation is very simple and does not require a belief in any religion or philosophy to be effective. Its purpose is to reach a state of mental calmness and control that allows the highest degree of mental focus and yet remains empty of thought. It is no coincidence that this state also defines the elite performer during a peak performance or flow experience.

Research has shown conclusively that meditation is one of the best techniques for reaching a deep state of relaxation and for achieving single-minded concentration and focus. The mental discipline one develops through the practice of meditation is the same as that which is necessary for high-level performance, and the daily practice of meditation has been shown to have a significant positive impact on performance. Many top athletes and even entire sports teams have adopted daily meditation as a part of their training regimen.

Although there are dozens of meditation types, one of the most common employs a device, called a mantra, to focus the attention upon. It can be a single word such as "one," "warm," "calm," "om," "hu," "loose," "ease," "deep," or "peace". The meaning of the word is not particularly important, but it must make you feel comfortable and relaxed. Some practitioners focus on a picture, such as the complex geometric mandalas created for this purpose, and others will take a single idea or image and gently play with it, turning it around in their minds.

To start, pick a place and time where you will be completely undisturbed for about twenty minutes. Sitting is preferred since you are more likely to nap when lying down. After a few moments of breathing deeply and slowly while letting all tension go, place the attention lightly on the mantra and try to keep it there. Invariably the attention will begin to wander and other thoughts will fight for your attention, but patiently bring the attention back to the mantra each time. This can be a frustrating experience initially, but with practice, a state of great peacefulness and calm will be achieved, as well as a heightened state of awareness, mental clarity, and focus. There are two types of meditation that are particularly effective for performers: concentration upon the breath and observation of the mind.

Meditation on the Breath

While maintaining a feeling of peace and ease within the body, focus on the sensation and sound of the breath as it goes into and leaves the lungs. Although your objective is to keep the attention focused upon the breath, the mind will not remain silent for long. When you realize that you have been carried away by your thoughts, return to the here and now by placing your attention back on the breath. You may do this dozens of times in a single meditation exercise, but with practice, you will gain more power over your mind and eventually cease to be victimized by unwanted negative or unproductive thoughts. This dual-purpose exercise produces a calm body and disciplined mind, both characteristics of elite performers. It is worth your time.

Observation of the Mind

Another effective technique is that of observing the stream of thoughts as they flow through your consciousness. This exercise presumes that if we stop identifying ourselves with the mind and its creations, we will come in contact with the deepest part of our being: the point of awareness that exists when the mind has been stilled. The objective of this meditation is to watch your thoughts and emotions rise and fall while remaining an observer, unattached and unaffected by them. If you sit as if by a peaceful stream and watch your thoughts the moment they come into existence, you will be drawn powerfully into the here and now. An alternative exercise is to still the mind completely and become completely present and aware of everything around you in the moment. As before, your thoughts will lure you away from the moment again and again, but in time, this exercise will have a profound effect on your concentration and focus in performance.

Yoga and tai chi are forms of meditation, as is virtually any activity in which you focus your attention completely in the moment on what you are doing, including playing your instrument.

Self-Hypnosis

The practice of hypnosis as a therapeutic tool has been long recognized by the medical profession but has only recently been used to help athletes. It has great potential to help performers and should be part of any mental training program. Although researchers know what hypnosis can do, they have not reached a consensus on the exact nature of the hypnotic state. Generally speaking, it is a state of focused attention, deep relaxation, and heightened suggestibility that allows one to tap into the subconscious mind and bypass conscious barriers. Some individuals are more susceptible to hypnosis than others, and not everyone responds to hypnosis in the same way. According to Liggett (2000), the general techniques used for relaxation are similar to those used for self-hypnosis, and performers who are particularly susceptible to hypnosis might find themselves in a light trance when practicing relaxation techniques.

Hypnosis is useful for overcoming destructive personal habits, undesirable emotions such as phobias, and chronic anxiety such as the fear of performing. It is a very powerful tool that is not harmful or complicated. There are numerous materials on self-hypnosis available at bookstores and libraries, but they are of no use until they are applied.

Relaxation Techniques

There are several types of relaxation techniques, and they all seem to have a few main points in common. The first is that you must practice them regularly, preferably at the same time each day. Bedtime is a good choice, but it is important that you remain awake to complete the exercise. If your schedule will allow it, try taking some time during lunch or right before dinner, which will have the added benefit of energizing you for the remainder of the day or evening. The place you choose to do the exercise should be free of distractions and interruptions.

To begin, lie down and get as comfortable as possible, breathing deeply and slowly. Put your attention on your feet, and imagine that they are as heavy as lead, sinking into the bed, or that you are made of wax or butter and are melting on a comfortably hot beach. (The effective but time-consuming autogenic training techniques of Johannes Schultz stress the importance of imagining the sensations of heaviness and warmth when practicing relaxation techniques.)

As you feel the tension leave your feet, place your attention on your ankles, calves, thighs, abdomen and chest, gradually moving up to the shoulders, neck, head, and face. When completed, you should feel completely relaxed, peaceful, and at ease.

Progressive Relaxation

Given that anxiety and fear cannot exist in a body that is calm and relaxed, Edmund Jacobsen (1930, 1976) developed what are among the best-known and effective exercises for relaxation. His progressive relaxation (PR) techniques consist of contracting specific muscle groups or body parts (right arm, left arm, right leg, etc.), holding the tension for a few seconds, and then letting the tension go. When these techniques are practiced regularly, a performer can learn to identify and release unwanted tension from the body, a practice that will become automatic over time.

Ronald M. Suinn (1976) has streamlined Jacobsen's technique, calling it visual motor behavior rehearsal (VMBR). This technique is done for approximately twenty minutes initially, but the ability to reach optimum relaxation can take as little as five minutes once it is learned. Examples of PR scripts that one would follow are given in Liggett (2000, 27–32) and Williams (1998, 226–28). Elite athletes in virtually every field of athletics use these techniques, and they are worthy of further investigation and application by performing artists.

Triggers, Cues, and Anchors

There is a way to instantly recall the feeling of being completely relaxed and feeling good during periods of high stress. The first requirement is a trigger, cue, or anchor, which can be a word or sound, an image, a feeling, a touch—virtually anything you wish. What you choose will trigger the state of relaxation, and it must be associated or anchored to that sensation. We can anchor feelings of confidence, happiness, and relaxation just as easily as we can anchor feelings of fear.

Using the technique of anchoring, we can associate any internal state with an external trigger. We do it unconsciously all the time, but we can learn to do it consciously for our own benefit. A new student told his teacher that he had a history of playing poorly in public and did not believe that he had the ability to perform successfully. After some preliminary questions, the teacher learned that the student had a negative performance experience a few years earlier and from that time, he associated performing with a fearful, uncomfortable, and embarrassed state. The teacher asked him to recall a situation when he felt good about performing, and he remembered the times as a child when he had played for his family and received praise and encouragement. The teacher asked him to recreate and reexperience those pleasant feelings while squeezing his thumb and forefinger together for a minute. From this simple exercise, the student was able to overcome feelings of fear and discomfort by triggering an internal state of confidence and well-being by squeezing his thumb and forefinger.

Anchoring the Breath

Since breath control has always been a recommended method of stress reduction, one cue that works especially well in high-stress situations is to focus on breathing. To anchor this cue, get into the state of deep relaxation described earlier and then take a relaxed, deep breath. When you are comfortably full, release the air through a small opening in the lips. Do not push the air out, but remain relaxed, especially in the abdominal region, and let it flow out as if sighing in relief. This is a particularly effective cue for wind players as their inhalation and exhalation during performance will be anchored to a physically relaxed and peaceful state. After this technique has been practiced for some time, the body will immediately remember the relaxed state when you trigger it by sighing in this way. This is the principal technique that I use under stressful conditions, and it always works for me.

Whether we are conscious of it or not, anchoring is a part of our lives and happens regularly and automatically; the things that trigger powerful feelings or memories from the past are often as simple as a familiar aroma or a tune that we heard repeatedly during a period in our lives. With little effort we can use anchoring to consciously modify our behavior for our own benefit. Those interested in more detail on techniques should seek out books on neurolinguistic programming (NLP), materials on the Silva Mind Control System, and books by Anthony Robbins (1986, 1991).

Visualization

Many readers remember Mary Lou Retton, the petite American gymnast, as she prepared to race down the runway for a series of perfect scores in the vault that led to her gold medal win in the 1988 Olympics. Like many modern athletes, she was the beneficiary of advances in the area of sports psychology. Most of those who watched her stand for several seconds in preparation for the launch were unaware that she was going through a mental ritual that was designed to help her produce a perfect vault every time. Since these techniques are capable of consistently reproducing complex athletic movements, it makes sense that performers in the arts might also benefit from learning them.

Imaging It

Visualization, also called imaging or mental rehearsal, has long been used by top athletes as a powerful tool for programming the mind and body for success. There are two important principles underlying visualization techniques. The first principle is that mentally imaging an activity is, to some degree, equal to physically doing it. Researchers have discovered, for example, that athletes who are relaxed and visualizing themselves going through physical activity are actually subtly activating the muscle groups needed to perform that activity. To experience this phenomenon, take a pendant on a chain or a key on a thread and hold it between your thumb and forefinger. Looking down the length of it from above, align the pendant over the center of a cross drawn on a piece of paper, and remaining relaxed, keep it as still as you can. Without initiating any physical movement whatsoever, shut your eyes and clearly imagine the pendant swinging back and forth. Soon you will find the pendant swinging in the direction you have imagined.

This same principle has also been demonstrated in studies measuring the ability of a group of athletes to successfully complete tasks such as shooting baskets or throwing darts. Researchers found that the group that combined physical practice with mental practice (i.e. visualizing the task) did significantly better than the group that just shot baskets. Most surprising, a third group that only imagined shooting baskets but did not physically practice did nearly as well as the group that physically practiced. It is clear that mental rehearsal is, in some respects, very much like the real thing.

Fooling the Unconscious

The second important principle of visualization techniques is that the so-called unconscious mind does not know the difference between a real and an imagined experience. A performer whose confidence has been undermined by repeated failure can create success experiences using his/her imagination. These imagined experiences will be treated as real by the mind and can form a foundation to overcome negative mental habits caused by past failures. Self-doubt, fear of failure, and destructive self-criticism usually stem from a failure event, and many of us automatically assume that if we have failed before, we will fail again. But it is possible to short-circuit self-doubt and fear by basing our self-confidence on success, even if it is only imaginary success.

Practicing Visualization

Visualization techniques are easy, but they must be practiced regularly in order to be effective. It could be weeks before you will see results, but they will be well worth the small amount of effort you expend. Choose a time and place where you won't be disturbed, and completely relax your body as described earlier. If you are preparing for a performance, begin to see it in your mind in great detail. Imagine yourself backstage, calm, relaxed, but charged with energy. Imagine moving across the stage, hear the sound of the applause, and see your friends and family demonstrating their love and support. Take your position, breathing freely and deeply, and start to play. Actually hear yourself playing exactly the way you want the music to go. If this is difficult, imagine how your favorite trumpet player would sound, only you are doing the playing. If you have had performance problems in the past, it is imperative to imagine only the type of attitudes and emotions you wish to have. Do not replay any attitudes, feelings, or scenarios associated with failure. Studies have shown that using more than one sense to create the visualization will increase its effectiveness, so see it, feel it, hear and even smell it.

Some people prefer to see the event through their own eyes and some from a perspective outside the body. Imagine in detail how you wish to look and act, perhaps modeling players you respect. Make the pictures in your mind as big, bold, and colorful as you can. In the end, you will have created a clear picture of the performance exactly as you want it to go from beginning to end. Any problems you have had in real performances must be addressed by imagining in detail the outcome you desire. With this technique, you can create a set of "memories" that accurately reflect who you want to be and how you want to act. Countless studies have shown that imagining the event in this fashion can rapidly and effectively improve performance in ways that are largely beyond the conscious control of our minds. This technique really works.

Expectation and Emotion

In order for your visualization to become a reality, it must contain two very important elements: you must have the unshakable belief that what you imagine has already been granted to you, and it must be filled with emotion. You must absolutely believe that what you imagine for yourself is a reality; emotion is the catalyst that starts the process of change. By emotion, I mean the feeling of being excited that what you have imagined will be truly wonderful. Without these two elements, belief and emotion, your visualization is like an empty shell. Please do not neglect these two things from your visualization practice or you will be wasting your time. As Thomas Fuller said, "Seeing's believing, but feeling's the truth."

Mental Rehearsal

Mental rehearsal of the music you are learning can be done at any time, but doing it while you are taking a short break from practicing the instrument is especially wise as it has the added benefit of allowing your embouchure to recover. In this type of visualization, we are primarily using our aural rather than visual faculties to image the preferred outcome. This means that we imagine exactly how we want the music to sound in our minds. Combining the physical manipulation of the instrument, such as pushing the valves or keys while doing mental rehearsal, will strengthen the images and help you learn the new behavior quicker. It is very important that you don't simply play back in your mind the way you usually perform the music. In the difficult passages that you have never gotten right, rehearse the music in slow motion over and over in your mind until you can hear it exactly as you want it to go.

Many performers also imagine story lines, images, lyrics, feelings, or programs when they play particular pieces. This technique takes the mind off of the technical aspects of music and may help in the memorization of the piece.

Regularly using visualization techniques can easily become an automatic activity with repeated practice. It is especially important to stop the mind's habit of replaying and reinforcing failures of the past. The empowering practice of programming ourselves for success starts with the blueprint that we create with our imagination.

Affirmation and Self-Image

In his groundbreaking *Psycho-Cybernetics* (1960), plastic surgeon Maxwell Maltz described the difficulty some of his patients had believing that they were no longer ugly or disfigured. He realized that the concept of ugly or beautiful was not rooted in outward appearances, but in what they believed in their own minds. He found that having a patient look in the mirror each morning and recite certain phrases that would affirm new beliefs could change this image. When you look in the mirror each morning, tell yourself that you are confident, and good under pressure, and that you enjoy performing. When you truly believe it, it will be true for you.

We are usually not aware of the limitations we place upon ourselves or that are placed upon us by others. Scientists once thought it impossible for a human being to run a mile in under four minutes, yet as soon as Roger Bannister did the impossible, other athletes did the same, proving that it was more a psychological than physical barrier.

Great performers have a strong sense within themselves that they are completely capable of doing what needs to be done. Some are born with it, but most acquire it through experience or training. Affirmations are a simple but effective technique to change your personal beliefs about who you are and what you are capable of doing. Imagine yourself being any way you want to be, and then look yourself in the eye and make it so. Remember to do it with expectation and emotion.

Rehearsing Negative Images

Nearly everyone spends a certain amount of mental energy imagining negative outcomes to events in our lives. While driving home after a rehearsal for a recital that had not gone especially well, I suddenly realized that I was imagining myself playing poorly in the recital. I should have been doing just the opposite. When you catch yourself creating imaginary scenarios that have outcomes you don't want, stop and create a new one with an ending you like.

We will always find confirmation of our beliefs about ourselves in our daily life because we tend to interpret events to fit our beliefs. Performers who believe they are inadequate will unconsciously affirm this belief with statements they repeat over and over, such as "I always choke in performance" or "I'm not very good." Because of the strength that such affirmations have over behavior, they will begin to act as if these beliefs are true and look for confirmation of the truth of these beliefs in the events that happen in their lives. Of course, it is possible to frame any event in a positive or negative way and confirm virtually any point of view. Using the affirmation technique (see "Affirmation and Self-Image" in this chapter), tell yourself who you want to be and what you want to be true about yourself and your life. Very shortly you will be looking for and finding evidence all around you that what you believe about yourself is true.

Negative Thoughts and Beliefs

Many of the thoughts that pass through our minds while we are engaged in performance are detrimental. They distract our focus and concentration, degrade our confidence, and even disrupt automatic performance skill. Usually occurring as a reaction to events during performance, some negative thoughts are often completely irrational and make no sense when examined later. In addition to the usual fear, apprehension, and doubt, they include extreme perfectionism that imagines a little error as a disaster of major proportions and a sign that things are falling apart, or generalizations based upon past experiences or superstitions, such as believing that you cannot perform well except under certain specific circumstances. The best way to deal with these kinds of thoughts is to stop them as soon as you recognize their presence and replace them with positive affirmations such as "I am allowed a few errors—the audience will remember the music" or "I will make beautiful music today."

Often players will tie their self-concept or feelings of self-worth to their ability as a performer. They easily fall into depression if they play poorly and believe they are not a worthy person, which only makes things worse. We must always separate our performing ability from our concept of self-worth. Our level of skill attainment and artistry have no bearing on who we are as persons.

Confidence and Self-Esteem

Outstanding performers are confident, and in the sports science research there is a unanimous correlation between a performer's success and his/her self-confidence. The thoughts of successful performers are very different from performers who are not as successful.

One of the most critical components that make up confidence is what we think about ourselves and what we tell ourselves. Thoughts directly influence emotions and behavior. We have seen that there is a direct connection between the body and the mind. If we believe we have been cheated, for example, we become angry and the body undergoes a physiological change that represents anger. If we believe we are not up to a given task, then failure is assured, even if we have the skills and ability to succeed. Confident individuals regularly overcome seemingly insurmountable obstacles when guided by the unshakable confidence that success is not only possible but also a certainty. Simply believing we are capable of success is the key. Trumpet legend Doc Severinsen says "You just never think about missing a note. You have to have a positive visualization that it is all going to be right" (Green, 201).

In a recent study, the use of negative imagery in golf putting was shown to be detrimental to performance (Taylor and Shaw 2002). The researchers concluded that "outcome imagery influences performance through the mechanism of confidence" (612). This means that imagining a positive outcome, guided by confidence in one's ability, has a proven positive effect on success.

One need not be born with the trait of self-confidence; it is relatively easy to develop. Confidence is belief in one's ability, or self-assurance, and it includes such traits as optimism, or the conviction that things will turn out well, and self-efficacy, which is the absolute belief that one has the skills and ability to meet the specific task. One of the best ways to develop confidence is through positive self-talk.

Positive Self-Talk

Much of our thinking is an internal conversation wherein we describe our world to ourselves, reflect on the past, and plan for the future. This constant stream of thoughts can help our performance if they empower feelings and beliefs of confidence and success. Many elite athletes and performers use "pep talks" or positive self-talk as a form of self-coaching and encouragement. Studies involving Olympic athletes have shown that positive self-talk helps overcome cognitive anxiety, reinforces positive outcomes, and focuses concentration on the task at hand.

If we look outside of ourselves for support for a positive and confident self-image, we will likely be disappointed. With the exception of positive and constructive feedback from our teachers, friends, and loved ones, our daily life may more often present us with experiences that confirm our inadequacies and faults. Performers should not depend on feedback from outside of themselves to confirm positive beliefs and instill confident behavior. It must come from within each of us. Most of the great men and women in history overcame tremendous odds to succeed through a strong internal belief system that was usually not in agreement with the reality around them. Your experiences may have only confirmed that you are a poor performer, but that should not stop you from believing that you are growing, improving, and headed for great things. To give in to the "reality" around you is to lose all hope of ever reaching your goals or dreams.

Positive self-talk simply means saying things to yourself that empower you. It takes time and patience to stop the automatic habit of reinforcing negative memories, beliefs, and emotions. Self-talk should be used primarily to prepare for performance; performers who are completely immersed in an activity are at their best when they allow automatic processes to take over. Remember that too much thinking, whether good or bad, may disrupt the flow of performance.

Stress and Anxiety

Stress is neither positive nor negative. It is the body's reaction that determines whether a given stressor is good or bad. Researchers have identified three types of stress. Stress that energizes or motivates an individual, such as the feelings of excitement, anticipation, and nervousness that a confident performer may have as s/he steps on to the stage, is called *eustress*. When stress is so great that it overwhelms and frightens a performer and triggers fight-or-flight symptoms, it is called *distress* (or anxiety). *Neustress* refers to a neutral reaction to stressors or to stress that has no particular effect on a performer.

Distress generally has a negative impact on performance, as we have seen from the effects of fight or flight. Events that trigger distress are usually viewed by the performer as especially important, having an unpredictable outcome, or overwhelming and out of a performer's control. Eustress, on the other hand, occurs when a player feels capable of handling the event. It energizes and provides the edge that a performer needs to perform well.

State and Trait Anxiety

An individual may generally handle stress well but find that a given situation causes distress. This is known as *state anxiety*, and in this case, the player would be best served to employ relaxation techniques to lower his/her level of anxiety. Another individual may find s/he does not handle stress particularly well at any time, which is known as *trait anxiety*. In this case, the player would be best served to practice exercises over a period of time in order to learn to take control his/her anxiety and cease to be the effect of debilitating fear.

Performers in ensembles tend to have lower state anxiety than soloists, and greater performing experience leads to lower state anxiety. In addition, women, whose anxiety is affected by their perception of their own preparation, tend to have higher state anxiety than men, who are more anxious about their own success.

Somatic and Cognitive Anxiety

Somatic anxiety refers to stress's effects on the body, and *cognitive anxiety* refers to the mental effects of stress, which can include worrying about failure, fearing the unknown, doubting whether one is up to the task, or imagining undesirable outcomes. A moderate level of somatic anxiety is associated with high performance, but performers who exhibit higher levels of cognitive anxiety tend to perform more poorly than those with low levels of cognitive anxiety. In other words, high cognitive anxiety is related to the poorest performance, and low cognitive anxiety is related to the best performance. Too much worry or doubt hampers optimal performance, but a certain amount may help us keep our edge. In general, the best performers have learned to control cognitive anxiety and regulate their stress levels for optimal performance.

Cognitive and somatic anxiety can facilitate or debilitate a performer depending upon how the player views the event and handles stress. A given event may affect two performers in completely different ways: one performer may be overwhelmed by the task and another may view it as not only possible but also an exciting and desirable challenge.

Arousal

Arousal is the term that sports psychologists use to describe the body in a physiological state of readiness to perform. In this context the term does not refer to sexual arousal, but rather to the specific physiological changes initiated by the autonomous nervous system when we are under stress. A state of relaxed yet energized concentration is optimum for performance, but each of us is different. One person may need to be calmed down in order to reach the state of optimum arousal and another person may need to be "pumped up." An inappropriate level of arousal for the event usually causes poor performance, for it is possible to be either too aroused or not aroused enough. In order to perform with accuracy and consistency at the highest levels, it is critical for each of us to learn our optimal level of arousal, and to be able to know whether to reduce or increase the level by employing techniques to energize or relax the mind and body.

Over or Underarousal

A performer who is overly aroused for an event may exhibit signs of fight-or-flight syndrome. His/her mind will tend to be overly active, easily distracted, and difficult to focus, and negative emotions like anger, frustration, anxiety, or fear will easily rise in the consciousness. Because of excessive muscular tension, this performer may lose balance, timing, efficiency, and other critical aspects of psychomotor skill. To achieve optimum arousal, relaxation techniques are required.

On the other hand, there are times when a performer cannot seem to generate the energy or interest to do his/her best. This is most often the case during practice rather than performance situations. An underaroused performer may become bored or complacent, underestimate the difficulty of the task, fail to properly prepare, and lose concentration and focus. During underarousal, energy levels tend to be lower than needed for the task. The performer may feel fatigued, and physical skill will tend to lack precision and accuracy. To achieve optimum arousal, activation techniques are required.

Activation

If a performer exhibits a lack of interest and enthusiasm about a performance and feels mentally distracted, sluggish, and heavy, s/he may need to increase arousal in order to perform well. Imagery, word cues, and breathing are often used to energize the body. Imagining the body as a finely tuned machine that is smooth, powerful, and flowing is useful, as is self-talk, such as positive and affirming statements. Imagining that each breath is taking in energy and exhaling fatigue, or that the breathing apparatus is a generator of power, is also effective. Breathing forcefully and rapidly while pumping the arms and shouting positive words such as "Yes!" or "Go!" will energize the body very quickly. In general, acting as if energized will raise the body's state of arousal. Doc Severinsen uses push-ups to release tension and charge his body with energy (Green 206).

Eastern European athletes are taught self-activation through specific verbal phrases, breathing patterns, and imagery to change body state. In *Red Gold: Peak Performance Techniques of the Russian and East German Olympic Victors* (1988), Grigori Raiport discusses several activation techniques. These include inhaling for part of a phrase and exhaling on the italics, such as "Strength is *flowing into my body*" while visualizing a stream of vibrating energy being sucked into the lungs and flowing to every part of the body. The phrases are repeated two to four times. Other phrases include "I am *vigorous and alert*" and "I've had *a good rest.*"

Arousal Regulation Techniques

Achieving and maintaining a state of optimal arousal in performance first requires an understanding of one's best performance state, and this can only be determined through personal experience. The second requirement is an awareness of the body's state prior to and during the performance; this assessment will determine the need for arousal regulation techniques. One performer may need to decrease arousal, and techniques such as breath regulation, progressive muscle relaxation, meditation, and anchored states will be most effective. Another performer may need to increase his/her level, and for that, activation techniques would be used.

It is important to try to understand your own degree of nervousness in any given situation and observe how it affects your performance. When you learn the difference between too much, too little, and just right, you will be in a position to identify your pre-performance arousal state and possibly do something to change it if necessary.

Inverted-U Theory

A number of theories attempt to explain the relationship of arousal to performance, but the so-called "inverted-U theory" of Yerkes and Dodson (1908) is the one accepted by most researchers. This theory suggests that the highest levels of performance generally correlate with moderate levels of arousal. In other words, the athletes with only moderate levels of physiological anxiety performed the best, and athletes who had very high or very low levels of anxiety did not do as well. When this data is plotted on a graph, the result is an inverted-U or bell shape, with the moderate level of arousal (and highest level of performance) represented at the top of the curve and the lowest and highest levels of arousal (and worst performance) represented at the edges of the bell.

However, there are other factors to consider before accepting this rather general assumption. For example, researchers have found that the optimal performance of an easy task generally requires a higher level of arousal, but a difficult task requires a lower level. Further, an expert will tend to perform better at higher levels of arousal than a novice, who will require a lower level of arousal. The nature of the task itself must also be taken into account. For instance, a task requiring high levels of concentration and control, such as putting in golf, will require lower levels of arousal, but a task involving great strength and energy expenditure, such playing football, will require high levels of arousal.

Zone of Optimal Functioning

Yuri L. Hanin (1989) proposed an alternative to the inverted-U curve, arguing that every performer has a "zone of optimal functioning" (ZOF). In order to perform at the highest level, a performer must find his/her ZOF; poor performance is the result of arousal that is below or above this optimal zone. According to Hanin, some athletes will function best at a high level of arousal and others will function best at a low level, rather than the midpoint as predicted by the inverted-U theory. Some recent studies support this idea.

Attention and Concentration

Lapses in concentration may be the most common reason for the average player's performance errors, and improving concentration has been shown to have a positive impact on performance ability.

Attention can be thought of as the searchlight of our consciousness, illuminating those things we direct our awareness to, and concentration can be thought of as the facility that holds and focuses that light. It is generally believed that concentration is a skill that can be taught and developed, and this idea is supported by practitioners of meditation and thought-control techniques. (See "Performing in the Now" and "Meditation" in this chapter.)

According to Simons (1998), there are three areas where we may direct our attention during a performance: cognitively, or to our thoughts, decisions, emotions, and worries; somatically, or to the sense of the state of our body; and externally, to the information our senses receive from the world around us. The ability to control and hold attention varies from person to person and is also dependent upon the external stimulus, but the most important factor is what we decide to concentrate our attention upon.

When we perform, most of our actions are preprogrammed and automatic. If this were not the case, we would be overwhelmed with tasks, decisions, and thoughts that needed our attention. Like computer memory, we have a limited amount of attention available, and if most of it is given to one thing, less is available to handle other matters.

High-level performance requires a variety of types of attention, including direction of attention; breadth of attention from narrow "hard focus" to broad, "soft focus"; duration; and intensity. Concentrating the attention for long periods on a given task requires effort and discipline, especially if we have decided the task is boring. Quickly switching one's attention from narrow to broad and directing it instantly to various aspects of the performance is an important aspect of concentration. For example, a trumpeter performing a solo must actively interpret the music heard while reading the notation on the page, listen and react to the accompanist, and constantly scan the body to make quick performance decisions based on factors such as fatigue and difficulty of the immediate task. In addition, the attention may also be occupied with distractions such as thoughts about the audience, constant mental assessment of how well the performance is going, or panic about elements of the performance that are not going well. Often a player will pat him/herself on the back for playing well before the performance has ended, resulting in a concentration lapse that causes errors.

Arousal and Attention

Arousal has a direct impact on attention. Low arousal typically results in broad, general focus and high arousal results in narrow focus, which helps us concentrate on the performance. If arousal is too high, however, fight or flight is activated and concentration is adversely affected. Concentration errors frequently happen in low-arousal situations, such as when we are performing music that presents no challenge.

Among the best attention training exercises are those that rehearse focusing on a single object or thought, those that focus on stopping all thought, and those that rehearse changing the direction and focus of our attention. Meditation, visualization, and self-hypnosis are most highly recommended to improve concentration skills. Rehearsing music intended for performance while distractions are present is another way to learn to direct and focus the attention. I sometimes practice pieces I am preparing in front of the television. The extreme distraction tests my attention, simulating the worst possible conditions. When practicing in this fashion, I periodically give the TV my undivided attention, allowing rest and recovery from the instrument. I can practice for several hours this way with minimal physical and mental fatigue.

Sight-Reading Music

Learning to read music is similar to learning a language: we start with combinations of letters that form words, and then combinations of words that form sentences. Beginning music readers interpret notation at the letter or word level, but interpreting musical symbols in large chunks, like sentences, is the hallmark of the expert reader. (Transposition and interpreting chord changes are other cognitive skills that involve reading.)

Sight-reading, the ability to read music that has not been seen or heard before, is a learned cognitive skill that can be improved with practice. The primary goal of the sight reader is to play the music as perfectly as possible without stopping for any reason. Although it is desirable to interpret every symbol on the page, the sight reader should be primarily concerned with tempo and rhythm, followed by pitch and expression.

Through practice, larger and larger chunks of musical notation are automatically recognized as the symbols become familiar. Because expert sight readers see music symbols in groups, they are able to look ahead of the music they are playing. The common suggestion to "read ahead," however, is not a good strategy for the poor to mediocre sight reader, who usually can do no better than to focus his/her attention on what s/he is playing at the moment. For this reason, the best advice to a sight reader is to stay focused on what you are playing. Stilling the mind to halt fears and negative thoughts will improve sight-reading ability.

Individuals with dyslexia and other learning disabilities may have great difficulty reading music. For more information, see *Music and Dyslexia: Opening New Doors* by Tim Miles and John Westcombe and *A Soprano on Her Head* by Eloise Ristad.

Goal Setting

Goals are the achievement end points we establish for ourselves. They may be objective and measurable, such as reaching a specific level of proficiency in a task, or subjective, referring to emotional states or attitudes. They may be long or short term, difficult or easy, and specific or general.

Research has shown that goal setting is definitely effective in improving the performance of most tasks. Specific, measurable goals, such as "I will play this piece with no rhythmic errors," were rated more effective than general goals, such as "I will play well." Goals that were challenging but attainable were better than unrealistic, unattainable goals or goals that are too easily attained, but finding a balance between pushing too hard and not enough is sometimes difficult. Some research has suggested that the best strategy is a combination of short-term goals ("I will perfect this etude by Friday") with long-term goals ("I will increase my sixteenth-note single-tongue speed to MM=126 by the first of next month"). Bandura (1986) suggests that short-term goals are more effective because of the frequent evaluation of progress and sense of accomplishment. It is important to focus goals on your individual performance rather than on the outcome of an event over which you might not have any control. Establishing a target date for the accomplishment or completion of a goal is critical, as is writing the goal down and posting it in a visible place to ensure that it is worked on.

One of the most important steps after setting a goal is to plan specific strategies or approaches for attainment that are regularly evaluated and revised as necessary. Without this step, a goal could take a long time to reach or it may never be reached. Feedback about our progress toward a goal will help us understand where our efforts lie relative to the goal. It provides us with the knowledge that our efforts are helping us accomplish our goal or showing us that we need to change our strategy.

The most common goal-setting errors include setting too many goals, losing track of goals, failing to adjust one's goals to changing circumstances, and setting goals than are too general and not measurable.

Motivation

If we loved everything about our work and were constantly rewarded for our successes, it would be easy to remain highly motivated to achieve. Unfortunately, the real world seems to present us with unpleasant and unsatisfying tasks that offer little immediate reward. In the path of our desire to achieve often lie fatigue, health problems, personal problems, poor confidence, laziness, boredom, the perception of impossibly difficult tasks, frustrating setbacks, deadlines, and many other obstacles. How does a Lance Armstrong overcome incredible odds to win the Tour de France six times in a row? The answer is motivation.

Motivation covers a host of forces, both internal and external, that initiate, direct, and sustain behavior. It is associated with the proper arousal state, emotions, goals, and thoughts that lead to success. Two general types of motivation have received attention from researchers in recent years. *Extrinsic* motivation refers to behavior that is done as a means to an end, such as a musician who performs primarily for money or fame, and *intrinsic* motivation refers to behavior that is done purely for the satisfaction or enjoyment of doing it, such as a musician who just loves to play. Perhaps the most basic view of motivation is represented by the proverbial carrot and stick: sometimes we are motivated to avoid pain and sometimes we are motivated by the promise of pleasure. Both are a legitimate means to motivation. In fact, Atkinson's (1965) widely accepted theory of achievement motivation states that the personality factors that affect achievement are a combination and balance of two factors: the motive to move toward success and the motive to avoid failure. This means that the principal motivators of a high achiever are the capacity to feel pride in accomplishment and to feel shame in failure.

Recent research has concluded that competition (particularly winning) can increase intrinsic motivation more than noncompetitive situations, but situations that emphasize individual mastery rather than competition are even greater motivators. In other words, the desire for mastery of an artistic medium is generally a greater motivator than the desire to be better than everyone else. Nicholls (1989) classifies the two high-achievement personality types as the individual who is motivated to master a task for its own sake (task goal orientation) and the individual who is motivated to master a task to outperform others (ego goal orientation.) Both are viable approaches to motivation, and it is possible for one person to be task oriented in one environment, such as wanting to learn to play a musical instrument for the pleasure of it, and ego oriented in another, such as wanting to play tennis better than anyone else. It is interesting to note that the motivation of an intrinsically motivated individual is often lowered when extrinsic rewards are offered.

The highly motivated individual who has a sense of control over his/her life is able to continue pursuit of goals after experiencing setbacks and failure. This person has a strong belief that success is not only possible but inevitable. In addition, high achievers have an inner need to pursue excellence and feel pleasure and fulfillment in meeting challenging goals.

Bandura (1986) states that one of the most critical aspects of motivation is self-efficacy, or the strong inner conviction that we have the ability to perform a specific task. Confidence is usually based in our past successes, but we have seen that actively visualizing success combined with a positive belief in oneself can overcome the reality of past failures.

Mental Training Techniques as Part of Your Routine

Four areas should be part of every mental training program: visualization techniques, arousal control (including relaxation and activation techniques), thought control, and goal setting. Although experienced performing artists know very well the importance of mental factors on high-level performance, mental training techniques are not usually a part of musician's training the way they are for an athlete's. Athletic training incorporates a variety of techniques for competition readiness. Without them, months of training can be wasted in an instant by a substandard performance caused by lack of mental preparation. The same is true for artistic performance. Mental training is the glue that holds the pieces together, ensuring that a performer is able to fully utilize all of the preparation and hard work that has led to a given moment—the performance.

A Final Note

Some players seem to derive little pleasure from practice and are easily distracted or disinclined to apply themselves. In such cases, making an effort to view practice as an enjoyable and satisfying activity that produces positive results can help break up negative thought patterns that live in the practice room. Become aware of and stop any tendency to doubt your ability, to visualize failures or problems in the future, or to be mentally preoccupied with the past and future. Instead, put your attention fully on what you are playing and make it as beautiful as you can.

7

A Letter to My Students

Teaching the trumpet is a difficult task. The development and refinement of high-level psychomotor skill is a slow and frequently frustrating process. We teachers rely on our personal experience, training, and intuition to solve the problems that come into the studio each day. Every student has a unique pattern of physical and mental characteristics that must be explored and understood in order to properly prescribe workable solutions for the obstacles that halt forward progress. Not every ailment has an immediate solution, and a diagnosis may be a shot in the dark until more is known. For most situations, patience is the order of the day.

The ability to demonstrate on your instrument the desired musical product, even without uttering a single word of instruction, is generally regarded as an extremely important qualification of a fine teacher, but not every artist can teach. How we choose to teach is every bit as important as what we teach. Noting that there are many different ways to teach successfully, I would like to explain some of the principles that are the foundation for the way I work. The wonderful teachers to whom I owe so much shared these ideas with me, and now I pass them on to you.

- "It is my job to help you to become the best musician you can be." I am committed to helping you realize as much of your potential as possible during our time together. I will address your problems individually, giving each of you what you need to take the next step on your own path.
- "You are the only teacher you will ever have." I am a coach, a guide, a resource, or any number of roles according to your needs, but you must spend the time in the practice room required to apply what we have discussed in the lesson. Knowing about the trumpet intellectually is not the same as knowing it as reflex in your muscles and nerves. I cannot teach you how to play—you must do it alone. There are no shortcuts.
- "We learn through a process of imitation and trial and error." Musical expression is best learned through the imitation of that which we strive to become, so we must closely study the greatest practitioners of our art and apply the pertinent aspects of their lives and work. Experimentation with new techniques and ideas rarely leads to success immediately, so you must try over and over, modifying your approach until you succeed. Learning cannot occur without failure—there is no other way.
- "Repetition is the mother of all learning." Complex psychomotor skill is acquired through repetition. One of the most important aspects of high-level skill is the ability to perform a task with no conscious mental effort. This is called automaticity, and it can only be gained through repetition. The most efficient and effective method of learning any physical task is by repeating it slowly and perfectly until it is automatic.
- "It is not the instrument we must master, but ourselves." We must diligently address our areas of weakness and not blame any person, thing, or condition outside of ourselves for our inability to improve. Knowledge of our strengths and weaknesses is essential to growth, as this shows us where we need to direct our energies for maximum benefit.
- "I won't take credit for your success or your failure." I will play an important part in your growth, but you will do all the work and you are solely responsible for the outcome. I am proud of my students, but I will never claim credit for their successes, nor will I accept responsibility for their failures.
- "Take what you can use and leave the rest." I do not have all the answers, but I ask that you make a good-faith effort to apply the sug-

gestions we have discussed. If they don't work for you, we'll try something else. If you come across other ideas that are more effective, by all means use them, but running from one new thing to another without a sincere attempt at application will only lead to frustration.

- "Give without thought of reward." We can never really thank those who have helped us become what we are today, but we can pass on, in the same spirit, all that they have shared. Do not think that you will be given reward, credit, or even gratitude for your work with a student. Do it with love. There is no greater way to honor your teachers.

BIBLIOGRAPHY

Alcantara, Pedro de. *Indirect Procedures: A Musician's Guide to the Alexander Technique*. London: Oxford, 1997.

Anderson, Cat. *The Cat Anderson Trumpet Method*. Van Nuys, Calif.: Alfred, 1973.

Arban, Joseph Jean Baptiste Laurent. *Complete Conservatory Method*. Edited by Edwin Franko Goldman and Walter M. Smith. New York: C. Fischer, 1936.

Ash, D. W., and D. H. Holding. "Backward Versus Forward Chaining in the Acquisition of Keyboard Skill." *Human Factors* 32 (1990): 139–46.

Ashy, M. H., D. K. Landin, and A. M. Lee. "Relationship of Practice Using Correct Technique to Achievement in a Motor Skill." *Journal of Teaching in Physical Education* 7 (1988): 115–20.

Atkinson, John W. *An Introduction to Motivation*. Princeton, N.J.: Van Nostrand, 1965.

Autrey, Byron. *Basic Guide to Trumpet Playing*. Chicago: M. M. Cole, 1963.

Baldwin, David. "The Seven Secrets of Endurance." *International Trumpet Guild Journal* (Dec. 1996): 58.

Bandura, Albert. *Principles of Behavior Modification*. New York: Holt, Reinhart and Winston, 1969.

———. *Social Foundations of Thought and Action: A Social Cognitive Theory*. Englewood Cliffs, N.J.: Prentice Hall, 1986.

Barker, Sarah. *The Alexander Technique: The Revolutionary Way to Use Your Body for Total Energy*. New York: Bantam, 1981.

Barlow, Wilfred. *The Alexander Technique*. Rochester, Vt.: Healing Arts Press, 1990.

Benson, Herbert. *The Mind/Body Effect*. New York: Simon and Schuster, 1979.

Bernhardt, Roger, and David Martin. *Self-Mastery through Self-Hypnosis*. New York: Signet, 1977.

Bourre, Jean-Marie. *Brainfood*. Boston: Little, Brown, 1993.

Bragdon, Allen D., and David Gamon. *Brains That Work a Little Differently: Recent Discoveries about Common Brain Diversities*. New York: Barnes and Noble, 2000.

Brantigan, Thomas A., and Charles O. Brantigan. "Beta Blockade and Stage Fright, Looking Back." *International Trumpet Guild Journal* (May 1984): 20–22.

Brody, Janet E. "For Artists and Musicians, Creativity Can Mean Illness and Injury." *New York Times*, Oct. 17, 1989, C1, C12.

Brown, Christina. *The Book of Yoga*. Bath, U.K.: Parragon, 2002.

Brubeck, David William. "The Pedagogy of Arnold Jacobs." *TUBA Journal* (Fall 1991): 55–58.

Bruckner, Susan. *The Whole Musician: A Multi-Sensory Guide to Practice, Performance, and Pedagogy.* Santa Cruz, Calif.: Effey Street Press, 1998.

Brummett, Verna, ed. *Ithaca Conference '96: Music as Intelligence.* Ithaca, N.Y.: Ithaca College, 1997.

Bruser, Madeline. *The Art of Practicing: A Guide to Making Music From the Heart.* New York: Bell Tower, 1999.

Burke, Edmund R. *Optimal Muscle Recovery: Your Guide to Achieving Peak Physical Performance.* New York: Avery, 1999.

Bush, Irving R. *Artistic Trumpet Technique and Study.* Hollywood: Highland Music, 1962.

Callet, Jerome. *Superchops.* New York: Jerome Callet, 1987.

Carter, William. "The Role of the Glottis in Brass Playing." *Instrumentalist* (Dec. 1966). In *Brass Anthology*, 425–28. Northfield, Il.: Instrumentalist Company, 1987.

Chance, Paul. *Learning and Behavior.* 2nd ed. Belmont, Calif.: Wadsworth, 1988.

Chuen, Lam Kam. *Tai Chi.* New York: Fireside, 1994.

———. *The Way of Energy*. New York: Gaia, 1991.

Clarke, Herbert L. *How I Became a Cornetist*. Kenosha, Wisc.: Leblanc Educational Publications. Originally published: St. Louis, Mo.: Huber, c. 1934.

———. *Technical Studies for the Cornet*. New York: Fischer, 1912.

Colwell, Richard, and Carol Richardson, eds. *The New Handbook of Research on Music and Learning.* New York: Oxford, 1992.

Conable, Barbara. *How to Learn the Alexander Technique.* With William Conable. Columbus, Ohio: Andover, 1995.

Constable, George, ed. *The Trained Mind: Total Concentration*. Alexandria, Va.: Time-Life, 1988.

Cooper, Andrew. *Playing in the Zone.* Boston: Shambala, 1998.

Cox, Richard H. *Managing Your Head and Body So You Can Become a Good Musician*. Springfield, Mo.: Cox and Cox, 1999.

Cratty, Bryant J. *Teaching Motor Skills.* Englewood Cliffs, N.J.: Prentice Hall, 1973.

Csikszentmihalyi, Mihaly. *Flow.* New York: HarperCollins, 1990.

Culf, Nicola. *Musicians' Injuries: A Guide to Their Understanding and Prevention.* Guiford, England: Parapress, 1998.

Curtis, John D. *The Mindset for Winning.* La Crosse, Wisc.: Coulee, 1991.

Dale, Delbert. *Trumpet Technique.* New York: Oxford, 1965.

Darden, Ellington. *Living Longer Stronger.* New York: Perigree, 1995.

Diagram Group. *The Brain: A User's Manual.* New York: Putnam, 1982.

Dibbell, David G. "Can Surgery Improve Trumpet Playing?" *NACWPI Journal* (Fall 1978): 24–25.

———. "The Incompetent Palate: A Trumpeting Disaster." *International Trumpet Guild Journal* (Oct. 1977): 37–38.

Dienstfrey, Harris. *Where the Mind Meets the Body.* New York: HarperCollins, 1991.

Dorfman, H. A., and Karl Kuehl. *The Mental Game of Baseball.* Southbend, Ind.: Diamond Communications, 1995.

Dudgeon, Ralph T. "Credit Where Credit Is Due: The Life and Brass Teaching of Donald S. Reinhardt." *International Trumpet Guild* (June 2000): 27–39.

Dufty, William. *Sugar Blues.* Radnor, Pa.: Chilton, 1975.

Ericsson, K. A., R. T. Krampe, and C. Tesch-Römer. "The Role of Deliberate Practice in the Acquisition of Expert Performance." *Psychological Review* 100 (1993): 363–406.

Evans, Marc. *Endurance Athlete's Edge.* Champaign, Ill.: Human Kinetics, 1997.

Fadle, Heinz. *Looking for the Natural Way: Thoughts on the Trombone and Brass Playing.* Detmold, Germany: Edition Piccolo, 1996.

Farkas, Phillip. *The Art of Brass Playing.* Rochester, N.Y.: Wind Music, 1962.

———. *The Art of Musicianship.* Bloomington, Ind.: Musical Publications, 1976.

Faulkner, Maurice, and E. P. Sharpey-Schafer. "Circulatory Effects of Trumpet Playing." *British Medical Journal* (1959). Reprinted in *International Trumpet Guild Journal* (Feb. 1982): 22–23.

Fowler, Charles, ed. *The Crane Symposium: Toward an Understanding of the Leaning and Teaching of Music Performance.* Pottsdam, N.Y.: Pottsdam College of SUNY, 1988.

Fox, Fred. *Essentials of Brass Playing.* Pittsburgh, Pa.: Volkwein, 1976.

Frederiksen, Brian. *Arnold Jacobs: Song and Wind.* Edited by John Taylor. Gurnee, Ill.: Windsong Press Limited, 1996.

Gallwey, W. Timothy. *The Inner Game of Tennis.* New York: Random House, 1974.

———, and Robert Kriegel. *Inner Skiing.* New York: Random House, 1997.

Gardner, Howard. *The Theory of Multiple Intelligences.* New York: Basic Books, 1983.

———. *Multiple Intelligences: The Theory in Practice.* New York: Basic Books, 1993.

Gardner, Ned. "Dental Bonding: An Aid for the Embouchure." *International Trumpet Guild Journal* (Feb. 1986): 19–20.

Garfield, Charles A. *Peak Performance: Mental Techniques of the World's Greatest Athletes.* With Hal Zina Benett. New York: Warner, 1984.

Gelb, Michael. *Body Learning: An Introduction to the Alexander Technique.* New York: Henry Holt, 1987.

Gellatly, Angus, ed. *The Skillful Mind.* Philadelphia, Pa.: Open University Press, 1986.

Ghitalla, Armando. "Armando Ghitalla on Trumpet." Transcribed by Keith Clark. *Instrumentalist* (Nov. 1974): 72–75.

———. "Armando Ghitalla on Trumpet, (Part II)." Transcribed by Keith Clark. *Instrumentalist* (Dec. 1974): 73–75.

Gibson, Daryl, J. *A Textbook for Trumpet*. Minneapolis, Minn.: T. S. Dennison, 1962.

Gill, Diane L. *Psychological Dynamics of Sport and Exercise.* 2nd ed. Greensboro: University of North Carolina, 2000.

Goode, Michael I. *Stage Fright in Music Performance and Its Relationship to the Unconscious.* Oak Park, Ill.: Trumpetworks Press, 2003.

Gordon, Claude. *Brass Playing Is No Harder Than Deep Breathing.* New York: C. Fischer, 1987.

Gray, Judith A. *Dance Instruction*. Champaign, Ill.: Human Kinetics, 1989.

Green, Elmer, and Alyce Green. *Beyond Biofeedback*. New York: Dell, 1977.

Grindea, Carola, ed. *Tensions in the Performance of Music: A Symposium*. London: Kahn and Averill, 1987.

Guarneri, Mario. *Brass Basics and the BERP.* Audio (CD) www.berp.com.

Hanin, Yuri L. "Interpersonal and Intragroup Anxiety in Sports." In *Anxiety in Sports: An Interactional* Perspective, edited by Dieter Hackfort and Charles D. Spielberger, 19–28. New York: Hemisphere, 1989.

Hanson, Fay. *Brass Playing: Mechanism and Technic.* New York: C. Fischer, 1968.

Haynie, John James. *How to Play High Notes, Low Notes, and All Those In Between.* New York: Colin, 1988.

———. *A Videofluorographic Presentation of the Physiological Phenomena Influencing Trumpet Performance.* Denton, Texas: North Texas State University School of Music, [1968?].

Hergenhahn, B. R. *An Introduction to Theories of Learning.* Englewood Cliffs, N.J.: Prentice Hall, 1988.

Herrigel, Eugen. *Zen in the Art of Archery.* New York: Vintage, 1971.

Hewitt, James. *Relaxation*. Chicago: NTC, 1994.

Horn, Thelma, ed. *Advances in Sport Psychology.* 2nd ed. Champaign, Ill.: Human Kinetics, 2002.

Horvath, Janet. *Playing (less) Hurt: An Injury Guide for Musicians.* 2002. www.playinglesshurt.com.

Howard, James A. "Temporomandibular Joint Disorders, Facial Pain, and Dental Problems in Performing Artists." In *Textbook of Performing Art Medicine,* edited by Robert T. Sataloff, Alice G. Brandfonbrener, and Richard J. Lederman, 111–69. New York: Raven, 1991.

Howard, Pierce J. *The Owner's Manual for the Brain*. Charlotte, N.C.: Leornian Press, 1994.

Hunt, Norman. *Guide to Brass Playing.* Dubuque, Iowa: W. C. Brown, 1978.

Hyams, Joe. *Zen in the Martial Arts.* Los Angeles: Tarcher/Houghton Mifflin, 1979.

Hymes, Alan. "Respiration and the Chest: The Mechanics of Breathing." In *Science of Breath*, by Swami Rama, Rudolph Ballentine, and Alan Hymes, 18–44. Honesdale, Pa.: Himalayan Institute, 1998.

Irons, Earl D. *Twenty-Seven Groups of Exercises for Cornet and Trumpet*. San Antonio, Texas: Southern Music, 1938.

Jackson, Susan A., and Mihaly Csikszentmihalyi. *Flow in Sports.* Champaign, Ill.: Human Kinetics, 1999.

Jacobs, Arnold. Taped lectures from the 1987 Summer Arnold Jacobs master class at Northwestern University. Unpublished, collection of Loren Parker.

Jacobsen, Edmund. *Progressive Relaxation.* Chicago: University of Chicago Press, 1930.

———. *You Must Relax.* New York: McGraw-Hill, 1976.

Jacoby, Don. *Jake's Method: The Trumpet Method of Don "Jake" Jacoby.* Denton, Texas: Jacobotz, 1990.

Johnson, Harry W. "Skill = Speed x Accuracy x Form x Adaptability." *Perceptual Motor Skills* 13 (1961): 163–70.

Johnson, Keith. *The Art of Trumpet Playing.* Ames: Iowa State University Press, 1981.

———. *Brass Performance and Pedagogy.* Upper Saddle River, N.J.: Pearson Education, 2002.

Karter, Karon. *The Complete Idiot's Guide to the Pilates Method.* Indianapolis, Ind.: Alpha, 2001.

Kelly, Kevin. "The Dynamics of Breathing: A Medical/Musical Analysis." With Arnold Jacobs and David Cugell. In *Brass Anthology,* 1004–10. Northfield, Ill.: Instrumentalist Company, 1987.

Kerr, Robert. *Psychomotor Learning.* Philadelphia, Pa.: Saunders College Publishing, 1982.

Kirschenbaum, Dan. *Mind Matters: Seven Steps to Smarter Sport Performance.* Carmel, Ind.: Cooper, 1997.

Kochan, Andrew. "Treating the Pain of Playing Musical Instruments." *International Musician* (Aug. 2003): 9.

Kohut, Daniel L. *Musical Performance: Learning Theory and Pedagogy.* Champaign, Ill.: Stipes, 1992.

Kriegel, Robert, and Marilyn Harris Kriegel. *The C Zone: Peak Performance under Pressure.* Garden City, N.Y.: Anchor/Doubleday, 1984.

Krüger, Irmtraud Tarr. *Performance Power.* Translated by Edward Tarr. Tempe, Ariz.: Summit Books, 1993.

Kubistant, Tom. *Performing Your Best: A Guide to Psychological Skills for Achievers.* Champaign, Ill.: Life Enhancement, 1986.

Kurz, Thomas. *Science of Sport Training: How to Plan and Control Training for Peak Performance.* Island Pond, Vt.: Stadion, 1991.

Laban, Rudolf von, and F. C. Lawrence. *Effort.* London: Macdonald and Evans, 1947.

Lederman, Richard J. "Neurological Problems of Performing Artists." In *Textbook of Performing Art Medicine,* edited by Robert T. Sataloff, Alice G. Brandfonbrener, and Richard J. Lederman, 111–69. New York: Raven, 1991.

Lidor, Ronnie, and Michael Bar-Eli, eds. *Sport Psychology: Linking Theory and Practice.* Morgantown, W.Va.: Fitness Information Technology, 1999.

Lieberman, William B., and Robert C. Jones. "Dental Appliances as an Aid to Brass Playing." In *Brass Anthology*, 584–85. Northfield, Ill.: Instrumentalist Company, 1987.

Liggett, Donald R. *Sport Hypnosis.* Champaign, Ill.: Human Kinetics, 2000.

Lind, Ekard. *Exercises for Musicians.* Translated by Keith Harris. Arlington, Va.: Plucked String, 1987.

Lipp, Charles. "Arnold Jacobs' Master Class." Transcribed notes from the 1990 Arnold Jacobs Master Class at Northwestern University. http://trumpet.dana.edu/pedagogy/jacobs.html.

Livingston, Michael K. *Mental Discipline: The Pursuit of Peak Performance.* Champaign, Ill.: Human Kinetics, 1989.

Loehr, James E. *The New Toughness Training for Sports.* New York: Plume, 1994.

MacBeth, Carlton. *Original Louis Maggio System for Brass.* Burbank, Calif.: Aven, 1985.

Maltz, Maxwell. *Psycho-Cybernetics.* Englewood Cliffs, N.J.: Prentice Hall, 1960.

Mann, Stanley. *Triggers: A New Approach to Motivation.* Upper Saddle River, N.J.: Prentice Hall, 1987.

Markham, Ursula. *Visualization.* Rockport, Mass.: 1993.

McFarlane, Stewart. *The Complete Book of T'ai Chi.* New York: DK, 1997.

McKenzie, Robin. *Treat Your Own Neck.* Lower Hutt, New Zealand: Spinal, 1998.

Méndez, Rafael. *Prelude to Brass Playing.* New York: C. Fischer, 1951.

Mikesky, Alan E. "Strength Training." In *Encyclopedia of Sports Science,* edited by John Zumerchik, 471–87. New York: Simon and Schuster/Macmillan, 1997.

Miles, Tim R., and John Westcombe, eds. *Music and Dyslexia: Opening New Doors.* London: Whurr, 2001.

Milhollan, Frank, and Bill E. Forisha. *From Skinner to Rogers: Contrasting Approaches to Education.* Lincoln, Neb.: Professional Educators Publications, 1972.

Millman, Dan. *How to Succeed in Sport and Life: Transforming Training into a Path of Discovery.* New York: MJF, 1999.

Monaghan, Patricia, and Eleanor G. Viereck. *Meditation: The Complete Guide.* Novato, Calif.: New World Library, 1999.

Montgomery, Kate. *Carpal Tunnel Syndrome: Prevention and Treatment.* San Diego, Calif.: Sports Touch, 1993.

Morehead, Twanette. "Dentures, Braces, Overlays, and Brass." In *Brass Anthology,* 952–54. Northfield, Ill.: Instrumentalist Company, 1987.

Mortenson, Gary. "The Extraction of Wisdom Teeth: Information on Procedures and Problems." *International Trumpet Guild Journal* (Feb. 1990): 19–23.

Morton, Paul. "Ray Mase: Trumpet in Our Time." *International Trumpet Guild Journal* (Jan. 2003): 33–37.

Mueller, Herbert. *Learning to Teach Through Playing: A Brass Method.* Reading, Mass.: Addison-Wesley, 1968.

Murphy, Michael, and Rhea A. White. *In the Zone: Transcendent Experience in Sports.* New York: Penguin, 1995.

Nelson, Boris, and Anne Alexander. "An Interview with Maurice André." In *Brass Anthology*, 733–34. Northfield, Ill.: Instrumentalist Company, 1987.

Nelson, Florence, ed. "Megumi Kanda: Sliding Her Way into Music." *International Musician* (Aug. 2003): 21.

Nicholls, J. G. *The Competitive Ethos and Democratic Education.* Cambridge, Mass.: Harvard University Press, 1989.

Nideffer, Robert M. *The Inner Athlete: Mind Plus Muscle for Winning.* New York: Crowell, 1976.

Noble, Clyde. *The Psychology of Cornet and Trumpet Playing.* Missoula, Mont.: Mountain Press, 1964.

Norman, Donald A. *Learning and Memory.* San Francisco: Freeman, 1982.

Norris, Richard. *The Musician's Survival Manual: A Guide to Preventing and Treating Injuries in Instrumentalists.* St. Louis, Mo.: MMB, 1993.

Novak, Janice. *Posture, Get It Straight!* New York: Perigree, 1999.

O'Connor, Joseph, and Ian McDermott. *NLP.* London: Thorsons, 2001.

Olson, R. Dale. "Trumpet Pedal Register Unveiled." In *Brass Anthology*, 360–61. Northfield, Ill.: Instrumentalist Company, 1987.

Orlick, Terry. *In Pursuit of Excellence.* Champaign, Ill.: Human Kinetics, 1980.

Paull, Barbara, and Christine Harrison. *The Athletic Musician: Playing Without Pain.* Lanham, Md.: Scarecrow, 1997.

Pfund, William A. *The Trumpeter's Pedagogical Guide*, 1992. William A. Pfund, 35629 Weld County Road #41, Eaton, Colo. 80615.

Phelps, Joseph F. "Dystonia: A Trumpeter's Story." *International Trumpet Guild* (March 2002): 45–46.

Planas, Jaime. "Further Experience with Rupture of the Obicularis Oris in Trumpet Players." *International Trumpet Guild Journal* (May 1996): 22–24.

———."Rupture of the Obicularis Oris in Trumpet Players (Satchmo's Syndrome)." *International Trumpet Guild Journal* (Dec. 1982): 12–14.

Porter, Maurice M. *The Embouchure.* London: Boosey and Hawkes, 1967.

Proctor, Robert W., and Addie Dutta. *Skill Acquisition and Human Performance.* Thousand Oaks, Calif.: Sage, 1995.

Raiport, Grigori. *Red Gold: Peak Performance Techniques of the Russian and East German Olympic Victors.* New York: Putnam, 1988.

Ramacharaka, Yogi. *The Science of Breath.* Chicago: Yogi Publication Society, 1905.

Reinhardt, Donald S. *The Augmented Encyclopedia of the Pivot System.* New York: Colin, 1973.

Restak, Richard. *The Brain.* New York: Bantam, 1984.

———. *Receptors.* New York: Bantam, 1994.

Ristad, Eloise. *A Soprano on Her Head: Right-Side-Up Reflections on Life and Other Performances.* Moab, Utah: Real People, 1982.

Robbins, Anthony. *Awaken the Giant Within.* New York: Fireside, 1991.

———. *Unlimited Power.* New York: Fawcett Columbine, 1986.

Roehmann, Franz L., and Frank R. Wilson, eds. *The Biology of Music Making: Proceedings of the 1984 Denver Conference.* St. Louis, Mo.: MMB, 1988.

Sanborn, Chase. *Brass Tactics.* Toronto: Chase Sanborn, 1997.

Sataloff, Robert Thayer, Alice G. Brandfonbrener, and Richard J. Lederman, eds. *Textbook of Performing Arts Medicine.* New York: Raven, 1990.

Scherer, Lon. *Practicing.* Goshen, Ind.: Pinchpenny, 1988.

Schlossberg, Max. *Daily Drills and Technical Studies for Trumpet.* New York: M. Baron, 1938.

Schneiderman, Barbara. *Confident Musical Performance: The Art of Preparing.* St. Louis, Mo.: MMB, 1991.

Schuman, Joel S., Emma Craig Massicote, Shannon Connolly, Ellen Hertzmark, Bhaskar Mukherji, and Mandi Z. Kunen. "Increased Intraocular Pressure and Visual Field Defects in High Resistance Wind Instrument Players." *Opthamology* 107, 1 (Jan. 2000): 127–33.

Schwartz, Martin F. *Stutter No More.* New York: Simon and Schuster, 1991.

Severson, Paul, and Mark McDunn. *Brass Wind Artistry.* Athens, Ohio: Accura Music, 1983.

Sherman, Roger. *The Trumpeter's Handbook.* Athens, Ohio: Accura, 1979.

Simon, Harvey B., and Steven R. Levisohn. *The Athlete Within.* Boston: Little, Brown, 1987.

Simon, Tamar. "Practice Makes Perfect, But So Does Taking Breaks." August 12, 1997. Discovery Channel Canada. www.exn.ca/Stories/1997/08/07/01.asp.

Simons, Jeff. "Concentration." In *Case Studies in Applied Sport Psychology*, edited by Mark A. Thompson, Ralph A. Vernacchia, and William E. Moore, 89–104. Dubuque, Iowa: Kendall/Hunt, 1998.

Singer, Robert N., Heather A. Hausenblas, and Christopher M. Janelle, eds. *Handbook of Sport Psychology.* 2nd ed. New York: Wiley, 2001.

Sivananda Yoga Center. *The Sivananda Companion to Yoga.* New York: Simon and Schuster, 1983.

Sloboda, John A. *Generative Processes in Music.* New York: Clarendon, 1988.

———. "What Is Skill?" In *The Skillful Mind*, edited by Angus Gellatly, 16–37. Philadelphia: Open University Press, 1986.

Snell, Howard. *The Trumpet.* Isle of Man, Britain: Rakeway, 1997.

Sommer, Bobbe. *Psycho-Cybernetics 2000.* With Mark Falstein. Englewood Cliffs, N.J.: Prentice-Hall, 1993.

Spaulding, Roger W. *Double High* C *in 37 Weeks.* 5th ed. Anaheim, Calif.: High Note Studios, 1995.

Spencer, Frederick J. *Jazz and Death.* Oxford: University of Mississippi Press, 2002.

Spilka, Bill. *Chops.* New York: Colin Publishing Company, 1990.

Stamp, James. *Warm-Ups + Studies.* Moudon, Switzerland: Éditions BIM, 1978.

Stevens, Chris. *Alexander Technique.* Rutland, Vt.: Tuttle, 1987.

Stewart, M. Dee. *Arnold Jacobs: Legacy of a Master.* Northfield, Ill.: Instrumentalist, 1987.

Stoner, Roger. "Hearing Impairment—My Journey." International Trumpet Guild Journal (October 2001): 69, 71.

Suinn, Richard M. "Psychology in Sports: Methods and Applications." *Psychology Today* (July 1976): 38–43.

Suzuki, Shin'ichi. *Nurtured by Love.* Translated by Waltraud Suzuki. New York: Exposition Press, 1969.

Swami Rama, Rudolph Ballentine, and Alan Hymes. *Science of Breath*. Honesdale, Pa.: Himalayan Institute, 1998.

Swanwick, Keith. *Music, Mind, and Education*. New York: Routledge, 1988.

Taylor, J. A., and D. F. Shaw. "The Effects of Outcome Imagery on Golf Putting Performance." *Journal of Sport Sciences* 20 (2002): 607–13.

Thompson, James. *The Buzzing Book*. Moudon, Switzerland: Éditions BIM, 2001.

Thompson, Mark A., Ralph A. Vernacchia, and William E. Moore. *Case Studies in Applied Sport Psychology.* Dubuque, Iowa: Kendall/Hunt, 1998.

Thurmond, James M. *Note Grouping.* Camp Hill, Pa.: JMT Publications, 1982.

Tolle, Eckhart. *The Power of Now.* Novato, Calif.: New World Library, 1999.

Truax, Bert. *Bert's Basic Brass.* (DVD) www.berttruax.com.

Tutko, Thomas, and Umberto Tosi. *Sports Psyching: Playing Your Best Game All of the Time.* New York: Tarcher, 1976.

Van Nagel, C., Edward J. Reese, Mary Ann Reese, and Robert Siudzinski. *Mega Teaching and Learning.* Portland, Ore.: Metamorphous Press, 1985.

Wann, Daniel L. *Sport Psychology.* Upper Saddle River, N.J.: Prentice Hall, 1997.

Weast, Robert D. *Brass Performance.* New York: McGinnis and Marx, 1961.

———. *Famous Trumpet Players.* Johnston, Iowa: Brass World, 1998.

———. "A Stroboscopic Analysis of Lip Function." In *Brass Anthology*, 337–39. Northfield, Ill.: Instrumentalist Company, 1987.

Weeks, John, ed. "Transparent Man with a Horn." *North Texan* 19, 5 (Oct. 1968): 7–9.

Weisberg, Arthur. *The Art of Wind Playing.* New York: Schirmer, 1975.

Werner, Kenny. *Effortless Mastery: Liberating the Master Musician Within.* New Albany, Ind.: Jamey Aebersold Jazz, 1996.

Widdowson, Rosalind. *The Joy of Yoga.* Garden City, N.Y.: Doubleday, 1983.

Williams, Jean M., ed. *Applied Sport Psychology: Personal Growth to Peak Performance.* Mountain View, Calif.: Mayfield Publishing Company, 1998.

Williams, Jean M., and Dorothy Harris. "Relaxation and Energizing Techniques for Regulation of Arousal." In *Applied Sport Psychology,* edited by Jean Williams, 225–30. Mountain View, Calif.: Mayfield Publishing Company, 1998.

Wilson, Frank R. "Mind, Muscle and Music: Physiological Clues to Better Teaching." Teachercraft, Bulletin 4. Elkhart, Ind.: Selmer, 1981.

Winter, James H. *The Brass Instruments: Performance and Instructional Techniques.* Boston: Allyn and Bacon, 1964.

Yerkes, R. M., and J. D. Dodson. "The Relation of Strength of Stimulus to Rapidity of Habit-Formation." *Journal of Comparative Neurology and Psychology* 18 (1908): 459–82.

Young, Gene. *Embouchure Enlightment.* Denver: Tromba, 1977.

Zaichkowsky, Leonard D., and Wesley E. Sime, editors. *Stress Management for Sport.* Reston, Va.: AAHPERD, 1982.

Zi, Nancy. *The Art of Breathing.* New York: Bantam, 1986.

Zilbergeld, Bernie, and Arnold A. Lazarus. *Mind Power: Getting What You Want Through Mental Training.* New York: Ivy, 1987.

INDEX